EVERYTHING YOU NEED TO KNOW ABOUT EVERYTHING YOU NEED TO KNOW ABOUT

EVERYTHING YOU NEED TO KNOW ABOUT EVERYTHING YOU NEED TO KNOW ABOUT

Your world, and everything around it, in a nutshell

Daniel Tatarsky

Illustrated by Steve Russell

THUNDER BAY
P·R·E·S·S

San Diego, California

Thunder Bay Press
An imprint of the Baker & Taylor Publishing Group
10350 Barnes Canyon Road, San Diego, CA 92121
www.thunderbaybooks.com

Published in the United Kingdom in 2011 by Portico Books,
10 Southcombe Street, London W14 0RA
An imprint of Anova Books Company Ltd.

Library of Congress Cataloging-in-Publication Data

Tatarsky, Daniel.
   Everything you need to know about everything you need to know about : your world,
and everything around it, in a nutshell / Daniel Tatarsky.
       p. cm.
  Includes index.
  ISBN-13: 978-1-60710-358-5
  ISBN-10: 1-60710-358-3
  1. Handbooks, vade-mecums, etc. I. Title.
  AG106.T38 2011
  031.02--dc22
                              2011008233

1 2 3 4 5 15 14 13 12 11

Printed in China

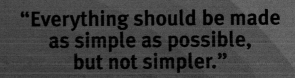

"Everything should be made
as simple as possible,
but not simpler."

Albert Einstein *(1879–1955)*

Contents_

03.0 The Living Earth_

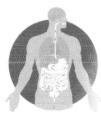

04.0 Humans_

Contents_ *cont.*

Introduction_

How is it possible for the contents of this book to live up to the title?

Let's start by knocking some things on the head. *Everything You Need to Know About Everything You Need to Know About* is not going to help you find your keys (they're probably in the door), explain why your first girlfriend dumped you (a lucky escape for you in all probability), or why everything that is so tasty is also so unhealthy (just live with it). What this book will attempt to do is give you the essential information about this planet, the universe beyond it, and all the things—both living and inanimate—that make it so unique and wonderfully special.

Research has shown that when people go to art galleries they spend, on average, three times longer reading the art's accompanying caption than they do looking at the art itself. Further research has shown that we humans retain visual information in our long-term memory quicker than the written word. These two pieces of research seem contradictory at first, but when you think about it, they actually prove each other.

Our brains can take in a picture, remember it, and even understand it really quickly, but the written word needs *processing*. It takes time for us to absorb information and digest it. The written word requires our brain to do a lot more work if we ever want to retrieve the information and put it to use again. In effect, what people usually do is read something, convert it into pictures in their head, and then, if it is of interest, try to remember it. So when we look at the *Mona Lisa*, we don't need to stare at her indescribable smile for hours to take it in (we only need a few seconds for that), but to retain the details of *who* painted it (come on, you know the answer to that one), when the artist was born, and how long it took—all that takes a little while longer.

It is this dichotomy that we are trying to harness in these pages. Each page, each nugget of information is delivered illustrated, taking advantage of all the exciting ways in which information can now be presented. At a single glance, you will get to the heart of the facts and your brain will process everything more quickly, then file the information away so that it is easily retrievable when you next need it for a conversation about, for example, atoms. Accompanying the charts, timelines, diagrams, and graphs are those captions that we all love to read, so that you get the bigger picture, too.

This book is for the geek in all of us who just wants to know how many people speak Chinese. It's for the big kid that needs to find out what was the largest dinosaur (and just how huge it was!). It's for the history nut who needs to know the date that Archduke Ferdinand was assassinated, and what were the small increments that led to a world war.

Everything You Need to Know About Everything You Need to Know About will take you from the big bang all the way up to—and just beyond—the Big Crash. It covers a lot of ground and there are a lot of exciting things to discover, so we better get started . . .

p.s. Any **bold text** in this book signals the introduction of a key point, person, or concept, which we hope might inspire you to delve further and discover even more than you need to know about everything you need to know about.

Chapter 01.0 Time & Space_

01.1 Before the Bang_

Until only very recently, the feeling among scientists was that *nothing* existed before the big bang—hence the relative emptiness of this page.

However, since **Albert Einstein** published his *Theory of General Relativity* (1915), and with recent advances in scientific debate (most notably quantum physics), there are now countless theories about what may have existed *before* the big bang. Unfortunately, there is just not enough space here to describe it in effective detail, and indeed what do we *really* know about it, after all?

All we can be sure of is that this tiny black dot—which represents the **entire universe** and contains everything you'll *ever* need to know about—is about to get a whole lot bigger.

(Dot not to scale.)

01.2 The Big Bang_

The big bang, otherwise known as when it all began, took place around 13.7 billion years ago. Because of its name, most people imagine—as we have done here—that the big bang was an immense, almighty explosion. However, it wasn't. Instead, it was a **rapid expansion of matter, energy, and gases**. The model of the big bang theory is built on the premise that the universe still appears to be expanding today, and it is from this expansion that scientists have been able to calculate, give or take a few million years, when the universe came into existence.

Many people forget that the big bang is only a theory, but it is currently by far the most popular and widely supported theory. The **observable evidence** for how everything began collected to date supports many other theories, including, of course, that it was created by one or more gods.

Something to Think About . . .

Sir Fred Hoyle is commonly accepted as the person who coined the phrase "big bang" in 1949. This must have been a source of irritation, as he was a strong opponent of the theory. Instead, Hoyle was an advocate of the "steady state" theory and only came up with the "big bang" tag to give a name to a theory he disagreed with.

In the Beginning

How the universe was created—according to **the world's six leading religions**.

Almost every religion has, written within its scriptures, a theory of how we all got here. The unifying element is the presence within these doctrines of a superior being, **the Creator**. Since science has provided proof of the big bang, as well as other explanations of our existence and evolution, religions—one might think— would have to accept defeat. But no, faith is still a powerful force.

Be it the Bible, the Koran, or the Torah, there are arguments within their pages that allow the believer to **question the science**. As there is not enough room here for their entire texts, here are their views on how everything got started.

Christianity ✝
2.4 billion followers

"In the beginning God created the heavens and the earth. And the earth was without form, and void . . . God said, 'Let there be light!'"
Bible, Genesis 1:1

Buddhism ☸
500 million followers

Followers of Buddhism believe in the theory of evolution and have **no theory** regarding the creation.

Something to Think About . . .

The Jedi religion, based on the beliefs of the Jedi Knights in the *Star Wars* films, was officially recognized as a religion in the UK in 2001. The Jedi church has chapters in England, Poland, Canada, and the United States.

Sikhism
26 million followers

"One universal creator God.
The name is Truth. Creative being personified.
No fear. No hatred. Image of the undying,
beyond birth, self-existent."
Guru Granth Sahib

Hinduism
900 million followers

"When the Brahman is born, the first
sound he makes is Om, from this all
creation comes."
The Bhagavad Gita

Judaism ✡
16 million followers

"In the beginning God created the heavens and
the earth. And the earth was without form,
and void . . . God said, 'Let there be light!' "
Torah, Genesis 1:1

Islam ☾★
1.15 billion followers

"It is He who created for you all of that which is on
the earth. Then He directed Himself to the heaven,
(His being above all creation), and made them seven
heavens, and He is knowing of all things."
Koran, Surat Al-Baqarah 2:2

The Composition of Our Universe_

The principle of the **conservation of energy** states that matter can be neither created nor destroyed, it can only be transformed. The essence of this implies that everything that is currently in the universe has always been there and will always be.

The problem is that since the big bang, we now know that the universe has been **expanding**. This means that the amount of **dark matter** as a percentage of the whole has increased, and it is still increasing.

Atoms, e.g., those of planets, stars, etc., make up just 4.6 percent of the universe. Dark matter accounts for 23 percent and dark energy 72 percent. Dark matter is basically stuff we can't see but which has mass. It is not really understood, but even less is known about **dark energy**. No one really knows what dark energy is, even though it accounts for nearly 75 percent of the universe. NASA has even set up a mission—the Joint Dark Energy Mission—which will attempt to figure it out.

Something to Think About . . .

Our knowledge of the universe is minimal, mainly because we just do not have the capability to travel, or even see far enough to figure things out. Research into what is beyond the universe, or what came before it, is really only carried out by philosophers because it is so far beyond the realms of current scientific reach.

Dark energy *72 percent*

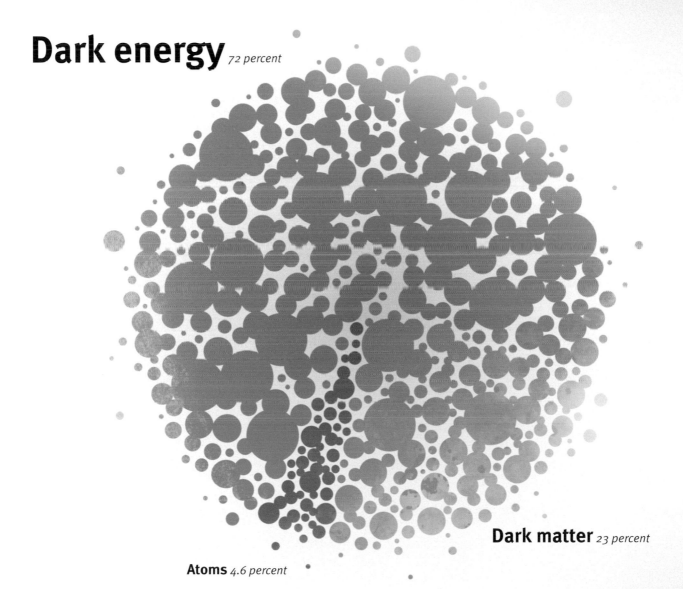

Dark matter *23 percent*

Atoms *4.6 percent*

01.5 The Known Galaxies_

A galaxy is a collection of stars, interstellar matter, dust, gas, and dark matter, held together as a distinct entity by **gravitational force**. The number of stars in a galaxy can vary from a few million up to several trillion. Earth is in a solar system that forms part of a galaxy called **the Milky Way**.

In the known universe, there are estimated to be at least a **hundred billion galaxies**, but it is impossible to determine the exact number.

With advances in telescopes, it has been possible to see galaxies that are millions of light-years away. Some of these galaxies have been named, such as **Hoag's Object**, which is a ring-shaped galaxy 600 million light-years away.

The Milky Way

Something to Think About . . .

The Milky Way is about 100,000 light-years in diameter. If you laid Milky Way chocolate bars from one end of the galaxy to the other, everyone on Earth would have to eat 6,813,000,000 of them every day (assuming we all lived to be 100) in order to consume them all.

It's a Fact . . .

Deep space was opened up to us with the launch of the Hubble Space Telescope in 1990. The telescope orbits Earth every ninety-seven minutes and beams images to several science instruments thanks to its Cassegrain reflector—a unique type of lens configuration.

A telescope works not by magnifying things but by collecting more light than the eye can. The Hubble Space Telescope's advantage over earthbound telescopes is that it is positioned above Earth's atmosphere, which distorts and filters out much of the light.

The universe

01.6 The Sun_

Earth sits in one of an infinite number of solar systems within the universe, and we refer to it simply as "the solar system." At the center of all solar systems is a star; we call our star "the Sun."

The Sun is **made up entirely of gas**, most of which is sensitive to magnetism and is known as plasma. The two main chemical elements that make up the Sun are **hydrogen** (72 percent of its mass) and **helium** (26 percent). The energy of the Sun is created by nuclear fusion within its core. This is when two nuclei combine to form a single nucleus. This fusion converts nuclear matter into energy. The temperature at the surface of the Sun is 10,000°F; at the core it is over 27,000,000°F.

The Sun contains most of the solar system's mass (99.8 percent); it is 330,000 times the mass of Earth, which in terms of relative difference is equivalent to that between a tennis ball and four elephants. In terms of size, the Sun is 109 times bigger than Earth—imagine a ball at the center of a soccer field, with the center circle representing the Sun. In terms of volume, about 1,300,000 Earths would fit inside the Sun.

Something to Think About . . .

The Sun's light takes just over eight minutes to reach Earth. The light that illuminates your kitchen as you pour your morning cup of coffee actually comes from a point in time before you turned on the coffeemaker.

Earth 🌑

Size: *Diameter 870,000 miles*
Composition: *(By mass) Hydrogen 72%, Helium 26%, Oxygen 1%, Carbon 0.4%*

The Night Sky_

On a clear night, the sky is illuminated by a myriad of stars twinkling in far-off space. These stars' relative position to one another appears to remain constant, and so over the years astronomers have grouped them together into constellations, even though in most cases the stars are in fact many light-years apart.

By using a system akin to joining the dots, these unconnected stars create objects that can be understood and easily recognized. A familiar sight to most of us, the Big Dipper forms part of the Great Bear constellation, also called Ursa Major. Orion (the Hunter) and his belt are another group of stars easily seen by the naked eye.

Early astronomers believed that Earth was flat, with a revolving sky above it. It wasn't until around 570 BC that the ancient Greeks calculated that **Earth was a sphere**. The skies had been studied long before that—especially the Sun and Moon, and how their positions related to the seasons. This led to further research into the night sky and eventually **developed into astronomy** as we now know it.

Although Earth spins on its axis and travels around the Sun, there are some stars that you are unable to see from the Northern Hemisphere, and some you can't see from the Southern Hemisphere. If you imagine a line that starts from the South Pole and shoots straight out of the North Pole, there is a star known as Polaris, or the **North Star**. As Earth spins, this star appears not to move while all the other stars spin around it.

Something to Think About . . .

BPM 37093 is the name of a star that seems to have cooled and crystallized, thus creating the biggest known diamond. It is around 50 light-years from Earth, 2,486 miles in diameter, and has been nicknamed Lucy after the Beatles' song "Lucy in the Sky with Diamonds."

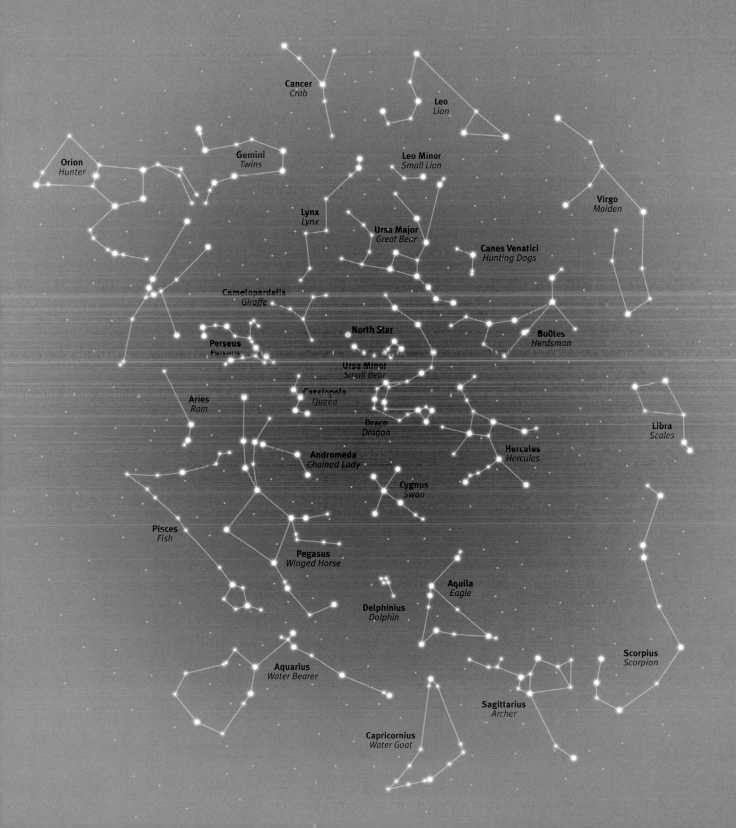

01.8 The Solar System_

Why is a year on Earth 365 days long? Or, more precisely, why is a year on Earth 365.25 days long?

It takes the Earth **365.25 days** to make one orbit around the Sun. We call this a year. But where does the measurement for a day come from? Well, it takes the Earth twenty-four hours to make a complete rotation around its axis; we'll call this one spin.

Okay, so a day is a spin and a year is an orbit. How do the planets compare?

The farther away a planet is from the Sun, the longer its orbit will take and hence the longer its year will last.

To put Pluto's orbit in perspective back here on Earth, if we go back one full orbit for Pluto, on Earth the year would be 1763 and the United States would still be a collection of English colonies.

What about the length of a day? If you have a bicycle with one little wheel and one big wheel, the small one rotates more quickly, but for the planets the opposite is generally true: **the larger a planet, the faster it spins**.

Something to Think About . . .

Here's a strange one. Venus takes about 225 days to orbit the Sun, but it takes more than 243 days to make one spin. What does that mean? In simple terms, on Venus a day is longer than a year.

Orbit time around the Sun (one year)—
given in Earth days

Pluto 90,465 days

Neptune 60,190 days

Uranus 30,684 days

Saturn 10,759 days

Jupiter 4,332 days

Mars 687 days

Earth 365.25 days

Venus 225 days

Mercury 88 days

01.9 Life on Other Planets_

Nobody knows how many planets there are in the universe, but based on the structure of our own solar system, there must be trillions. There are eight planets in our solar system, and one of them definitely has life on it. One in eight suggests good odds for life elsewhere. Even if Earth is the only planet out of nine million with life on it, the odds would still indicate that there must be life **somewhere else in the universe**. If this is the case, surely we must come across signs of another life-form at some point, right? Not necessarily.

The distances between galaxies, even solar systems, and the sheer number of them is such that for two life-forms to find each other "accidentally" would take a near miracle. It would be like one grain of sand on a beach in Miami trying to locate a specific grain on a beach thousands of miles away in Copacabana.

The other thing to note is that we always assume, especially in works of fiction, that if there are life-forms on a distant planet they are more intelligent than humans, and so therefore they will find us. While it is almost inconceivable that there isn't life somewhere else, there is no reason to suggest that we are not the most advanced. If everything in the universe comes from the big bang, then all the planets that are **capable of supporting life** have had as much time as each other to create it. All things considered, the probability is that there *is* life out there—but we will never find it.

Something to Think About . . .

In 1961 astrophysicist Frank Drake formulated the Drake equation. Generally accepted by the scientific community, this equation is a way of mathematically estimating the possible number of technologically advanced beings—intelligent enough to cross the vast void of space—that may exist in our galaxy. The equation looks like this:

$$N = R^* f_p n_e f_l f_i f_c L$$

Dr. Drake estimated that there could possibly be 10,000 alien civilizations in our own Milky Way galaxy.

The odds of alien life

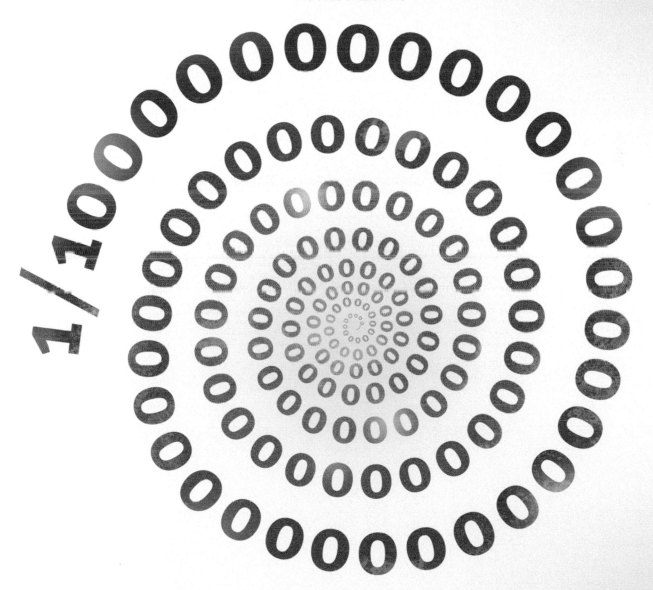

1/10000000000000...

The American astronomer and cosmologist Carl Sagan calculated that if you were to just spontaneously appear in the universe, the odds of you being anywhere near another planet—let alone one with life on it—would be "less than one in a billion trillion trillion," or 1 in 10^{33}.

The Planets_

Our solar system is in the Orion arm of the Milky Way. There are eight planets in our solar system, but the count has been as high as fifteen planets. This has changed as the definition of a planet has evolved.

At the general assembly of the **International Astronomical Union** in August 2006, resolution 5a set out a new definition of a planet:

(1) *A "planet" [1] is a celestial body that (a) is in orbit around the Sun, (b) has sufficient mass for its self-gravity to overcome rigid body forces so that it assumes a hydrostatic equilibrium (nearly round) shape, and (c) has cleared the neighborhood around its orbit.*

Venus

Average distance from the Sun:
67 million miles
Diameter: 7,523 miles
Gravity (compared to Earth): 0.88
Rotation time (in Earth days): 243.16
Speed: 1.29 mph

Days on Venus are longer than years.

Mars

Average distance from the Sun:
141 million miles
Diameter: 4,222 miles
Gravity (compared to Earth): 0.37
Rotation time (in Earth days): 1.0256
Speed: 171.51 mph

Olympus Mons is the solar system's largest known volcano.

Mercury

Average distance from the Sun:
36 million miles
Diameter: 3,030 miles
Gravity (compared to Earth): 0.38
Rotation time (in Earth days): 58.6461
Speed: 2.15 mph

Consisting mainly of iron, Mercury is the second-heaviest planet.

Earth

Average distance from the Sun:
93 million miles
Diameter: 7,926 miles
Gravity (compared to Earth): 1
Rotation time (in Earth days): 0.9972
Speed: 330.26 mph

Jupiter

Average distance from the Sun:
483 million miles
Diameter: 88,846 miles
Gravity (compared to Earth): 2.4
Rotation time (in Earth days): 0.4131
Speed: 8,961.26 mph

The Great Red Spot is a storm that has been raging for over 200 years.

As a result of part two of this resolution . . .

(2) A "dwarf planet" is a celestial body that (a) is in orbit around the Sun, (b) has sufficient mass for its self-gravity to overcome rigid body forces so that it assumes a hydrostatic equilibrium (nearly round) shape, (c) has not cleared the neighborhood around its orbit, and (d) is not a satellite.

. . . Pluto lost its status as a planet and is now classified as a **dwarf planet**.

Neptune

Average distance from the Sun:
2.79 billion miles
Diameter: 30,775 miles
Gravity (compared to Earth): 1.19
Rotation time (in Earth days): 0.6784
Speed: 1,890.15 mph

It was discovered because of an irregularity in Uranus's orbit that was created by Neptune's gravitational pull.

Saturn

Average distance from the Sun:
890 million miles
Diameter: 74,898 miles
Gravity (compared to Earth): 1.07
Rotation time (in Earth days): 0.4257
Speed: 7,330.83 mph

One of Saturn's moons, Titan, is larger than Mercury.

Uranus

Average distance from the Sun: 1.78 billion miles
Diameter: 31,761 miles
Gravity (compared to Earth): 0.9
Rotation time (in Earth days): 0.7166
Speed: 1,846.84 mph

Unlike all the other planets in the solar system, Uranus spins on its side in relation to the Sun.

01.11 Comets and Collisions_

As it orbits around the Sun once per year, Earth hurtles through space at 18.5 miles per second. The distance traveled on this orbital plane is 584,088,921 miles. Traveling through so much space so quickly, it is inevitable that every now and then something will get in our way—or will be on a collision course.

Each year, fewer than 1,000 meteorites hit Earth. Many of these objects burn up as they speed through our atmosphere. However, the larger meteorites that manage to get through and crash on land are no bigger than 33 feet in diameter.

NASA has developed a **monitoring and warning system** called SENTRY to keep an eye on anything more dangerous that could collide with Earth. SENTRY is an automated system that monitors the paths of near-Earth objects (NEOs) and plots their course for up to a hundred years ahead. If an object appeared that gave rise to a high risk on the **Torino scale** (right), we would hopefully have enough time to react.

Something to Think About . . .

The Tunguska impact is the only observed and verified major impact. It happened on June 30, 1908, in central Russia, but although it was seen by many people, there is no absolute certainty that this was, in fact, a meteorite.

10. Certain collision
*Collision is certain; global climatic catastrophe that may threaten
the future of civilization. Occurs once every 100,000 years.*

10

9. Certain collision
*Collision is certain; regional devastation for a land
Impact or the threat of a major tsunami for an
ocean impact. Occurs once every 100,000 years.*

9

8. Certain collision
*Collision is certain; localized destruction for an
impact over land or a tsunami if close offshore.
Occurs once every several thousand years.*

8

7. Threatening
*A very close encounter by a large object that poses an
unprecedented threat of a global catastrophe.*

7

6. Threatening
*A close encounter by a large object posing a serious threat
of global catastrophe. If less than three decades away,
governmental contingency planning is warranted.*

6

5

5. Threatening
*A close encounter posing a serious but uncertain threat of
regional devastation. If less than a decade away, governmental
contingency planning is warranted.*

4

4. Meriting attention by astronomers
*A 1 percent chance of collision capable of regional
devastation. The public is notified only if the possible
date of collision is less than a decade away.*

3

3. Meriting attention by astronomers
*A 1 percent chance of collision capable of localized
destruction. A close encounter.*

2

2. Meriting attention by astronomers
*A discovery of an object making a close pass
near Earth. Actual collision is very unlikely.*

1

1. Normal
*A routine discovery in which a pass near Earth is
predicted but poses no level of danger or concern.*

0

0. No hazard
The likelihood of collision is zero.

The Creation of Planet Earth in Four Easy Steps_

The Bible suggests that Earth (and everything in, on, and around it) was created in seven days—or six if you ignore the seventh day, when rest was required. Research has indicated that it actually took a little longer.

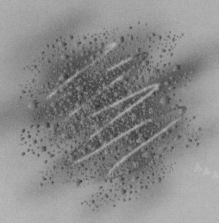

Step 1

Earth, the Sun, and the other planets in our solar system were formed through the gradual addition of layers due to the force of gravity from a nebula of gas and dust about 4.6 billion years ago (bya).

Step 2

In the period between 4.5 bya and 1 bya, the planet cooled so that now any water that is formed is not instantly evaporated. It is thought that much of our water came from comets—icy masses hurtling through space and crashing into Earth's surface. During this period, photosynthesis was possible.

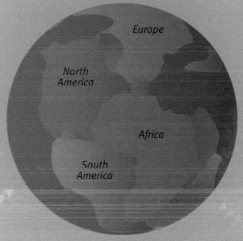

Step 3

About 500 million years ago (mya), life is now evident on the planet in the form of flora, and the existence of plant life creates more oxygen. It was from around this time onward that the dinosaurs developed and ruled the planet. At the time, the continents were joined in a single landmass called Pangaea, which slowly broke apart into today's continents. Most life on Earth was wiped out 65 mya when a massive asteroid hit—the dinosaurs' loss was humanity's gain.

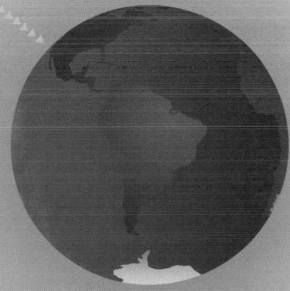

Step 4

After the dinosaurs died out and the dust settled (literally), the stage was set for the early development of humans. To get to this point, it had taken over four billion years since Earth first formed—a little more than six days.

Chapter 02.0　**Our World_**

The Structure and Composition of Earth_

Every student knows that Earth's surface is mainly water. In fact, it is just under 71 percent water, so land covers 29 percent of the surface. The surface area of the planet is 197 million square miles, so land covers 58 million square miles.

That tells us about the surface, but what about everything going on underneath? Earth is made up of five layers, a bit like a golf ball. As we start digging down through the outer layer, the **crust**, we come to the **upper mantle**. The crust is about 30 miles thick; it varies from place to place and is thinnest under the oceans. The crust under land comprises **granite**, **basalt**, and **diorite**, while under the oceans it is almost exclusively basalt.

The upper mantle is made up of iron and magnesium silicates. It goes down to a depth of 249 miles. Between the upper mantle and the crust is the **Mohorovicic discontinuity** (also known as the Moho), where seismic waves travel at a different and more rapid rate than they do in the crust or mantle.

The **lower mantle** comes next, and while the upper mantle is solid, the lower mantle is fluid. It extends down to a level of almost 1,864 miles and takes us to the **outer core**.

The outer core is molten lava made up of iron and nickel, and has an average temperature of 9,000°F. It surrounds the **inner core**, which is solid iron and nickel, and may reach temperatures as high as the Sun's surface.

Something to Think About . . .

Most of the information we have about what goes on beneath our feet is conjecture based on seismological surveys. No one has ever managed to drill through the crust into the mantle. As you get deeper, the temperature rises and the density of the rock increases—and we do not have equipment to cope with this.

Mantle ·······

The thickest layer of the planet—made up of moving rock, not lava—is about 1,800 miles thick. The mantle makes up about 84 percent of Earth's overall volume. The boundary between the upper mantle and lower mantle lies around 465 miles below the surface.

Crust

The crust is the layer farthest away from the hot inner core. Made up of rock, soil, and seabeds, its thickness is about 5 miles below the ocean and about 30 miles thick below the continents.

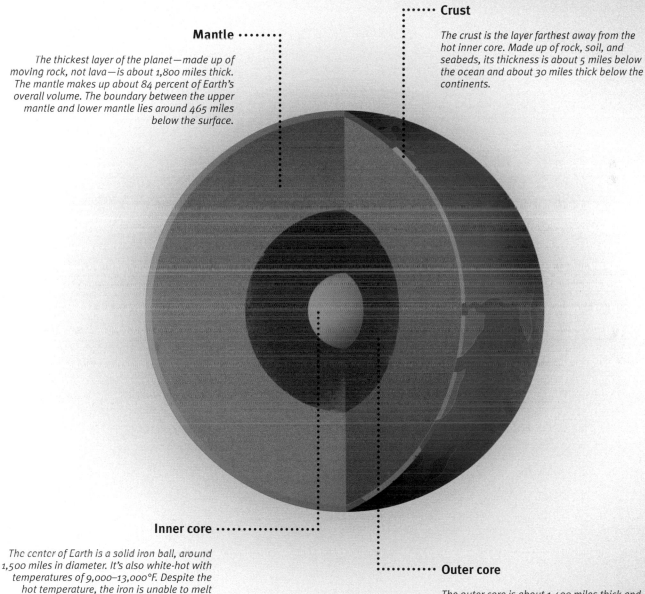

Inner core ·················

The center of Earth is a solid iron ball, around 1,500 miles in diameter. It's also white-hot with temperatures of 9,000–13,000°F. Despite the hot temperature, the iron is unable to melt due to the massive amount of pressure that is built up inside.

Outer core

The outer core is about 1,400 miles thick and surrounds the inner core. It is made up of liquid iron with significant amounts of nickel and sulfur. A lot cooler than the inner core, its temperature is estimated at around 5,000°F. The outer core creates Earth's vital magnetic field.

The Atmosphere_

Where does Earth's atmosphere end?

Earth's atmosphere is composed of those gases that surround the planet and are retained by its gravitational pull. There are **five main layers** that make up the atmosphere, and in descending order they are:

Layers of the atmosphere and their approximate altitude

Exosphere ·······································
Above 311 miles

Thermosphere ···································
53–311 miles
The Karman line lies in the atmosphere at 62 miles and defines the boundary between Earth's atmosphere and outer space.

Mesosphere ·····································
31–53 miles
The mesosphere rests above the maximum altitude an aircraft can fly.

Stratosphere ···································
7–31 miles
Weather balloons go up to around 22 miles.

Troposphere ····································
Surface–7 miles
Commercial airliners fly just below the top of this layer.

Something to Think About . . .

At an altitude of approximately 63,000 feet, atmospheric pressure is so low that water boils at 98°F, the temperature of the human body. This means that exposed body fluids like tears and saliva will begin to boil. This threshold is called the Armstrong limit after Harry Armstrong (1899–1983), who is known as the "father of space medicine."

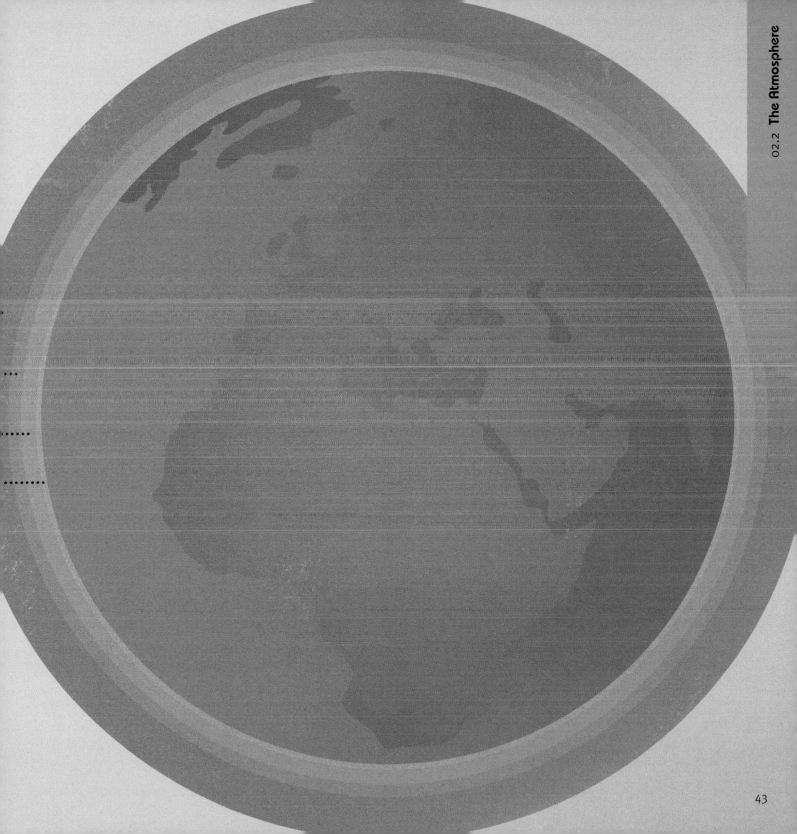

The Continents_

There are now seven continents: **Asia**, **Europe**, **Africa**, **North America**, **South America**, **Antarctica**, and **Oceania**. Two hundred and fifty million years ago, these continents were a single landmass called **Pangaea**.

Continents exist because the lithosphere, or the upper crust, is split into tectonic plates. These plates "float" around, which explains the change in the positions of the continents over time. Originally termed "continental drift," the implication was that this movement was quite random. However, as **plate tectonics** became the accepted theory, there are now four main ideas about what causes the movement of the continents. These are: convection currents in the upper mantle, gravity, Earth's rotation, and a combination of the three.

North America
Size: *9,536,723 square miles*
Population: *530,000,000*
Highest point: *Mount McKinley*
(20,320 feet)

South America
Size: 6,872,618 square miles
Population: *390,000,000*
Highest point: *Aconcagua*
(22,841 feet)

Something to Think About . . .

India is on a separate tectonic plate than the rest of Asia. It was the collision of these two plates that created the Himalayas around 55 million years ago, as the Indian plate traveled north and smashed into the Eurasian plate.

Europe
Size: *8,880,350 square miles*
Population: *728,000,000*
Highest point: *Mount Elbrus*
(18,510 feet)

Asia
Size: *19,189,277 square miles*
Population: *4,000,000,000*
Highest point: *Mount Everest*
(29,029 feet)

Africa
Size: *11,660,285 square miles*
Population: *885,000,000*
Highest point: *Mount Kilimanjaro*
(15,100 feet)

Oceania
Size: *3,320,479 square miles*
Population: *33,000,000*
Highest point: *Puncak Jaya*
(16,024 feet)

Antarctica
Size: *5,405,430 square miles*
Population: *0*
Highest point: *Mount Vinson*
(16,050 feet)

45

The Air We Breathe_

In the simplest terms, we are all able to live because we breathe out carbon dioxide, which trees and other plants breathe in. They then breathe out the oxygen that we breathe in, and so the cycle continues.

The astonishing thing is that the balance of the atmosphere is so stable. It goes to show that Earth is an incredible **self-regulating mechanism**. While the number of living things on the planet has increased, the amount of oxygen in the air has not gone down, and it is still perfectly balanced to support life on Earth.

Argon *0.934%*

Carbon dioxide *0.0314%*

Oxygen *20.9476%*

Something to Think About . . .

We don't think about breathing, we do it automatically, and we take for granted the supply of clean air. The World Health Organization estimates that two million deaths a year are attributable to air pollution.

Nitrogen *78.084%*

Other:

Neon *0.001818%*
Methane *0.0002%*
Helium *0.000524%*
Krypton *0.000114%*
Hydrogen *0.00005%*
Xenon *0.0000087%*
Ozone *0.000007%*
Nitrogen oxide *0.000001%*
Carbon monoxide *trace*
Ammonia *trace*

The Weather_

The seasons are what makes weather interesting and predictable, although not entirely. From a combination of Earth orbiting the Sun and Earth's axis being **slightly tilted**, we get seasons.

These two factors mean that, at different times of the year, any given place on Earth receives more or less sunlight each day. This affects temperatures and thus the weather. The variation in temperature between the two extremes becomes less the closer you are to the **equator**.

There are four seasons, the dates of which vary depending on where you are on Earth. The **Northern** and **Southern Hemispheres** experience the seasons at opposite times of the year.

Summer is when the Sun is at its strongest—or, rather, its most proximate—for the longest time. Winter is the opposite. Between winter and summer comes spring as the cold retreats and the land begins to warm up. Summer is followed by fall, when the plants and trees that bloom in summer begin to shed their leaves.

Largest snowflake recorded: *15 inches x 8 inches*
January 28, 1887, Fort Keogh, Montana

Most rainfall in 1 minute: *1.25 inches*
July 4, 1956, Unionville, Maryland

Most rainfall in 1 hour: *12 inches*
June 22, 1947, Holt, Missouri

Longest dry period: *173 months*
September 1903–January 1918, Arica, Chile

Something to Think About . . .

Nephelococcygia is the term applied to when people find familiar objects within the shape of a cloud.

Longest visible rainbow: *6 hours*
March 14, 1994, Wetherby, England

Highest temperature recorded: *136°F*
September 13, 1922, El Azizia, Libya

Deadliest tornado: *1,300 killed*
April 24, 1989, Manikganj, Bangladesh

Equator

Heaviest hailstone: *2.25 pounds*
April 14, 1986, Gopalganj, Bangladesh

Greatest wind gust speed: *253 mph*
April 10, 1996, Barrow Island, Australia

Most rainfall in 1 day: *6 feet*
January 7–8, 1966, Foc Foc, La Réunion

Lowest temperature recorded: *−128.6°F*
July 21, 1983, Vostok, Antarctica

02.6 The Power of Earthquakes_

What difference does one point on the Richter scale make?

Developed in 1935 by **Charles F. Richter** at the California Institute of Technology, the scale compares the magnitude of earthquakes. It goes from 1 to 10, with 1 being the weakest magnitude and 10 the strongest. An earthquake of magnitude 10 has never been recorded. The scale is based on logarithms, so each increase of one magnitude on the **magnitude scale** equates to a tenfold increase in **measured amplitude**.

For those lucky enough never to have been at the site of an earthquake when it happened, the following might help compare the forces; it is not meant to equate to them. If magnitude 1 is a punch in the stomach from a small child, magnitude 2 is a punch from a heavyweight boxer.

Something to Think About . . .

The largest recorded earthquake occurred in Chile in 1960. The magnitude of the earthquake was measured at 9.5, and it created a tsunami so huge that it raced across the Pacific Ocean and devastated Hawaii and even Japan with waves of up to 35 feet.

Magnitude 10
An equivalent force has not been witnessed in recorded history.

Magnitude 9
(Great) *Force of the 1960 Chilean earthquake.*

Magnitude 8
(Major) *Force of the 2008 Szechuan earthquake.*

Magnitude 7
(Strong) *Force of the 2009 Java earthquake and 2010 Haiti earthquake.*

Magnitude 6
(Moderate) *Can cause devastation for up to 100 miles in populated areas.*

Magnitude 5
(Light) *Equivalent force of the atomic bomb dropped on Nagasaki in 1945.*

Magnitude 4
(Minor) *Equivalent force of a small atomic bomb.*

Magnitude 3
(Micro) *An estimated 49,000 of these occur every year.*

Magnitude 2
Equivalent force of a conventional bomb blast in World War II.

Magnitude 1
Around 8,000 of these microearthquakes are recorded every single day.

02.7 Volcanoes_

Deep below Earth's crust there lurks hot, liquid rock, or **magma**. Like any fluid, magma seeks the route of least resistance—and as far as volcanoes are concerned, this is normally at the borders of the tectonic plates. Where magma finds a route out, usually via a random hole in the Earth's crust known as a **hot spot**, a volcano will form.

The timescales involved in the formation of a volcano vary wildly, but the best estimates are between 10,000 and 500,000 years, and they form over hundreds of separate eruptions.

Volcanoes generally fall into one of three categories: **active**, **dormant**, or **extinct**. The latter, as the name indicates, covers volcanoes that are regarded as unlikely to erupt again.

Active volcanoes are those that are currently erupting, are exhibiting signs to indicate that an eruption is still likely, or that have erupted in the last 10,000 years. The latter would appear to be a catchall, but because the gap between eruptions can cover a very long period, there is a need to remain cautious.

The difference between an active and a dormant volcano is very uncertain. In effect, a dormant volcano is one that may erupt again, but is not currently showing any signs that it might—yet it is one which no one is convinced can safely be classified as extinct.

The life cycle of a volcano generally follows these six stages:

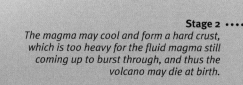

Stage 1 ·········
Magma finds a weakness, or gap, in the crust and pushes the rock and earth upward.

Stage 2 ······
The magma may cool and form a hard crust, which is too heavy for the fluid magma still coming up to burst through, and thus the volcano may die at birth.

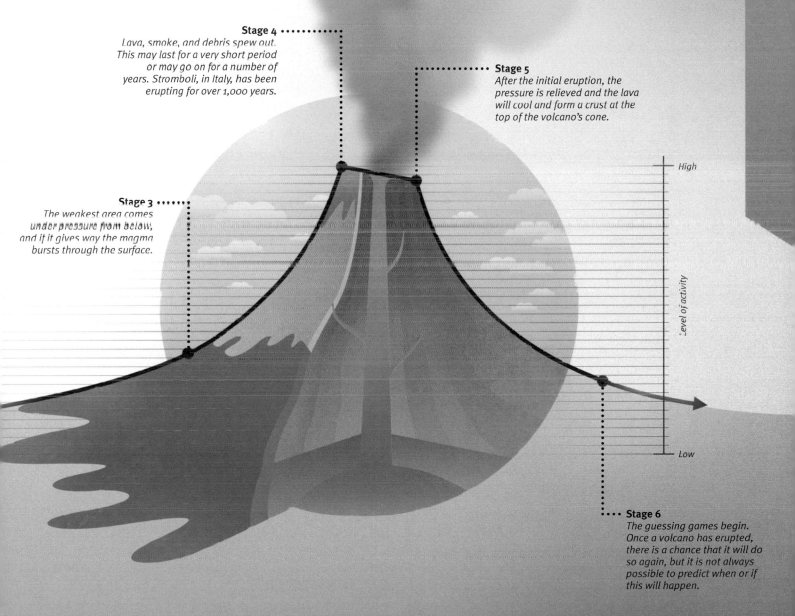

Stage 4 ·········
*Lava, smoke, and debris spew out.
This may last for a very short period
or may go on for a number of
years. Stromboli, in Italy, has been
erupting for over 1,000 years.*

Stage 5
*After the initial eruption, the
pressure is relieved and the lava
will cool and form a crust at the
top of the volcano's cone.*

Stage 3 ·······
*The weakest area comes
under pressure from below,
and if it gives way the magma
bursts through the surface.*

High

Low

Level of activity

Stage 6
*The guessing games begin.
Once a volcano has erupted,
there is a chance that it will do
so again, but it is not always
possible to predict when or if
this will happen.*

02.8 An Ocean World_

The first thing that is vital for life is water. When planet Earth first formed, it was dry and there was no water or moisture anywhere. So where did all the water come from?

Over the past 4.6 billion years, there have been many opportunities for water to arrive—or to be produced—on Earth. For many years it was believed that all the water that now forms our oceans was brought by **ice-bearing comets**, as the chemical signature of water in the oceans seemed to match that of all known comets.

However, modern studies now refute this. The most recent is an analysis of the **Hale-Bopp comet**, which was found to have much more "heavy hydrogen" than the water on Earth, thus making it unlikely that all our water came from comets alone. Some definitely did, but not all.

If this is the case, then the mystery continues . . .

Something to Think About . . .

Oceans are salty because the water that fills them up comes from rivers. As this water travels down to the sea, it picks up small amounts of salt from the riverbed. Once in the ocean, water is eventually removed by evaporation, but the salt is left behind.

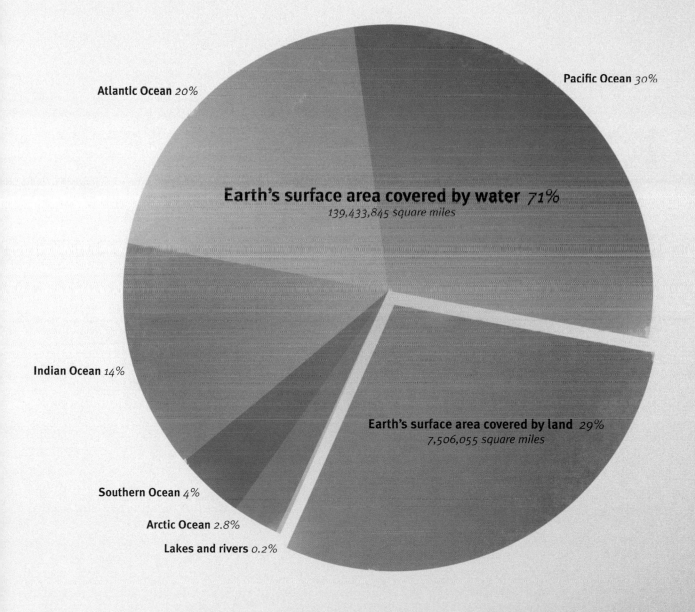

Pacific Ocean *30%*

Atlantic Ocean *20%*

Earth's surface area covered by water *71%*
139,433,845 square miles

Indian Ocean *14%*

Earth's surface area covered by land *29%*
7,506,055 square miles

Southern Ocean *4%*

Arctic Ocean *2.8%*

Lakes and rivers *0.2%*

The Water Cycle_

The water that exists on the planet today has been here as long, if not a little longer, than there has been life on Earth. The water cycle is the planet's **most effective recycling scheme**, and no matter what happens to it, water will always find its way back into the oceans so that the cycle can continue.

So what happens? First, the water in the oceans is heated up by the Sun. This causes **evaporation**, a process whereby the ocean's water changes from a liquid into a gas. The gas rises into the sky and, as the air temperature decreases higher up, the gas cools, **condenses**, and returns to a liquid state, thereby forming clouds.

As these clouds become bigger and heavier, they reach a point at which they can no longer remain in the air, and the water they contain must fall as **precipitation**. Wherever this falls, it will eventually find its way back to rivers, lakes, and oceans, and the process begins again.

In addition to providing us with drinking water, this cycle is vital for **maintaining the temperature** of the planet. As water evaporates and rises from oceans, it takes heat away from the planet's surface and regulates the atmosphere in much the same way as sweating keeps the body cool.

Something to Think About . . .

The deepest point in the oceans is the Mariana Trench in the Pacific Ocean, south of Japan. It goes down to a depth of nearly 7 miles. There is room for the whole of Mount Everest to fit in the trench, with 1.24 miles to spare.

01. The Sun evaporates ocean water
(evaporation)

02. This moisture rises to create clouds
(condensation)

05. Water returns to the oceans via rivers
(surface runoff and infiltration)

03. Clouds then move inland by wind

04. Clouds deposit water over land as rain or snow
(precipitation)

Lakes and Rivers_

While the vast majority of the world's water exists in the oceans (97 percent), our rivers and lakes, although holding only 0.2 percent of our water (the rest is held in glaciers, ice caps, and groundwater), are still important to our way of life. For many years, rivers provided a **source of energy,** and together with lakes, have always provided much of our drinking water. They have also been important for traveling and transporting materials, especially in areas where the land does not offer a viable alternative.

Lakes form where there is a **natural depression** in the landscape where water collects.

Rivers form when, due to the landscape, the water from lakes, springs, and small tributaries finds a common route down to the sea, another river, or another lake.

World's longest rivers

01. **Nile** *4,135 miles* (Africa)

02. **Amazon** *3,980 miles* (South America)

03. **Chang Jiang (Yangtze)** *3,917 miles* (China)

04. **Mississippi-Missouri** *3,870 miles* (United States)

05. **Yenisey** *3,434 miles* (Russia)

06. **Huang He** *3,395 miles* (China)

07. **Ob-Irtysh** *3,354 miles* (Russia)

World's largest lakes

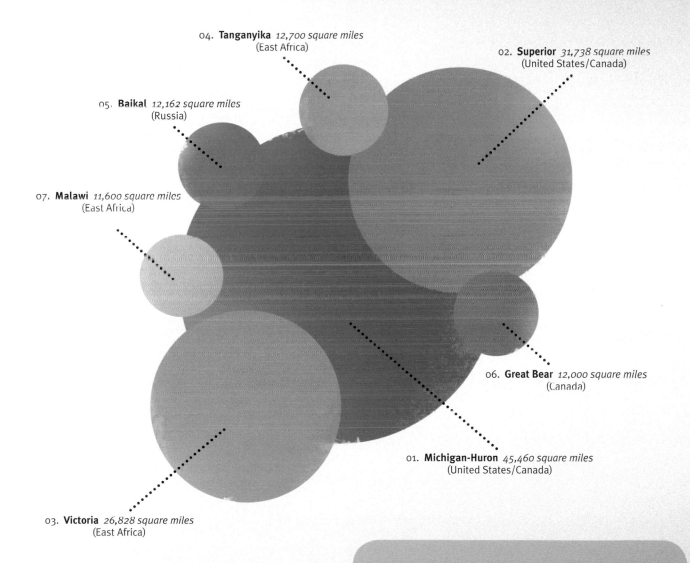

04. **Tanganyika** *12,700 square miles*
(East Africa)

02. **Superior** *31,738 square miles*
(United States/Canada)

05. **Baikal** *12,162 square miles*
(Russia)

07. **Malawi** *11,600 square miles*
(East Africa)

06. **Great Bear** *12,000 square miles*
(Canada)

01. **Michigan-Huron** *45,460 square miles*
(United States/Canada)

03. **Victoria** *26,828 square miles*
(East Africa)

Something to Think About . . .

The Roe River in Great Falls, Montana, is the shortest in
the world at a mere 200 feet.

The Ice Age Cometh_

We often refer to *the* Ice Age as though Earth has only ever had one such period. In fact, there have been many ice ages, and the one we now refer to as "the" Ice Age is merely the most recent. That ice age is called the **Pleistocene**, which reached its peak around 20,000 years ago and came to an end about 10,000 years ago.

An ice age is any period during which glaciers cover a large part of the planet; such a period has devastating effects on all living things. As the ice sheet spreads, most vegetation is destroyed as it is scraped off the surface by the advancing ice. Because **fauna** depends so much on **flora** for sustenance, animal life is forced to move to warmer areas, but as the ice age extends, these warmer areas diminish. Because so much of Earth's water becomes frozen, it cannot evaporate and produce rain, which means the planet becomes very dry. Even in these cold, dry, hostile conditions, certain creatures can flourish—as the **woolly mammoths** did during the last ice age.

The classic sawtooth pattern showing the cyclical nature of our planet's weather. This graph illustrates the slow but unstoppable arrival of ice.

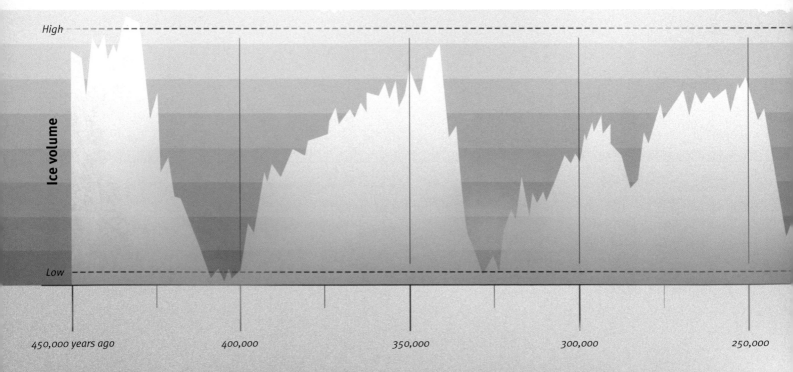

High

Ice volume

Low

450,000 years ago   400,000   350,000   300,000   250,000

The temperature of the planet—and in turn the reappearances of ice ages—is affected by some quirks of Earth's orbit and axis relative to the Sun. These were first reported by Serbian astrophysicist **Milutin Milankovic**. First, there is a 100,000-year cycle caused by variations in the orbit from more to less elliptical and then back again. Second, there is a 41,000-year cycle due to a quiver, or tilt, in the orbit of ± 1.5 degrees. Finally, there is a 21,000-year cycle caused by the combination of the first two factors. These combine so that the build-up to an ice age is slow but the end of it is abrupt, thus creating a classic, **sawtooth-shaped graph**, as seen below.

Something to Think About . . .

During the Pleistocene Ice Age, a third of the planet was covered by glaciers. Glaciers currently cover a tenth of the planet, which is why the period we are in now is sometimes referred to as a "mini ice age."

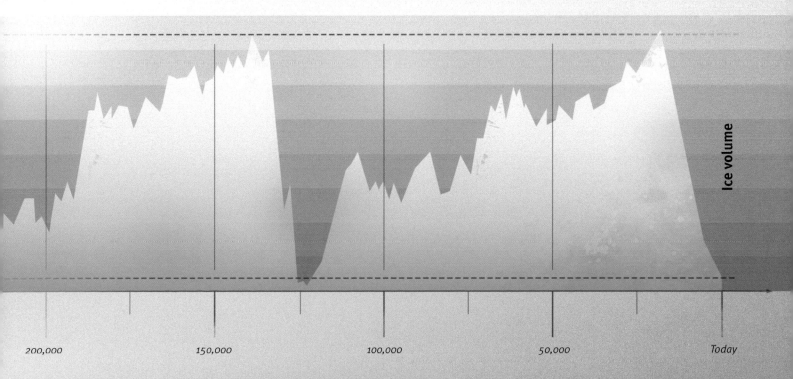

Ice volume

200,000   150,000   100,000   50,000   Today

Seven Natural Wonders of Our World_

Parícutin

What and where:
An active cinder-cone volcano in Michoacán, Mexico, 200 miles west of Mexico City. It has a height of 9,186 feet.
Best time to view:
Year-round

Parícutin is considered a unique natural wonder of the world, as humans witnessed its first eruption in 1943. It has been dormant since 1952.

Aurora Borealis
(Northern Lights)

What and where:
Occurring predominantly in Earth's ionosphere, the Northern Lights are caused by the colliding of ionized nitrogen atoms with solar-wind particles near Earth's magnetic North and South Poles.
Best time to view:
March–April and September–October

Renowned Italian scientist Galileo Galilei gave this phenomenon its Latin name. Aurora was the name of the Roman goddess of dawn.

Grand Canyon

What and where:
A deep chasm in Arizona that is 277 miles long and up to 18 miles wide in places.
Best time to view:
Year-round

The Grand Canyon was formed by the Colorado River and took 3,600,000 years to form. The river continues to erode and shape the canyon.

Victoria Falls

What and where:
Victoria Falls is the largest waterfall (based on width and height) in the world. Located in South Africa on the border between Zimbabwe and Zambia, and fed water directly from the Zambezi River, the waterfall is 5,600 feet wide and 360 feet high.
Best time to view:
May–October

Dr. David Livingstone, a famous Scottish explorer, gave the falls their name in the 1850s. It is also known locally as Mosi-oa-Tunya, which translates as "the Smoke That Thunders."

Mount Everest

What and where:
Mount Everest is the highest mountain above sea level and is located in the Himalayas on the border of Nepal and Tibet. Its peak stands at 29,029 feet. The mountain was formed 60 million years ago.
Best time to view:
October–November

In 1865 the mountain was named Everest after Sir George Everest, the British surveyor general of India. Tibetans know the mountain as Chomolungma, meaning "Holy Mother."

Great Barrier Reef

What and where:
The world's largest coral reef, situated off northeastern Australia (Queensland). The reef stretches over 1,600 miles and its 2,900 separate reefs are home to over an estimated 1.5 billion fish.
Best time to view:
June–October

With over two million tourists visiting the reef each year, it is one of the most-visited natural environments on Earth.

Harbor of Rio de Janeiro

What and where:
Also known as Guanabara Bay, the Harbor of Rio de Janeiro is found on the east coast of Brazil. It is the largest bay in the world based on water volume.
Best time to view:
September–October

The harbor is 19 miles long and 17 miles wide at its widest point. The harbor was formed by erosion from the Atlantic Ocean and is surrounded by unique mountain formations.

Chapter 03.0 The Living Earth_

Life as We Used to Know It_

What came first, the chicken or the egg?

It is the eternal question. One moment there was no life, the next there was. A miracle—perhaps. An accident of **a trillion coincidences** coming together to ignite the living world—probably.

Current theories indicate that the conditions that allowed life to begin are no longer present because the life created then has evolved, as has the atmosphere, and any such equivalent organism would not survive in the present conditions on Earth. It is difficult to replicate the planet as it was before life existed, so it is difficult to prove one way or another precisely how life began.

The predominant theories now all have elements of what is often called the **Oparin-Haldane hypothesis**. Russian biochemist Aleksandr Oparin and British-born geneticist John Haldane worked independently but came up with, in essence, the same idea—that life began in a **"primordial soup"** in which organic compounds went through various changes to create more complex molecules.

Something to Think About . . .

Prokaryotes are the most primitive cells on the planet, but without them no other form of life would exist. In the same way that the longest journey starts with a single step, the journey toward all life on Earth began with the humble prokaryotes.

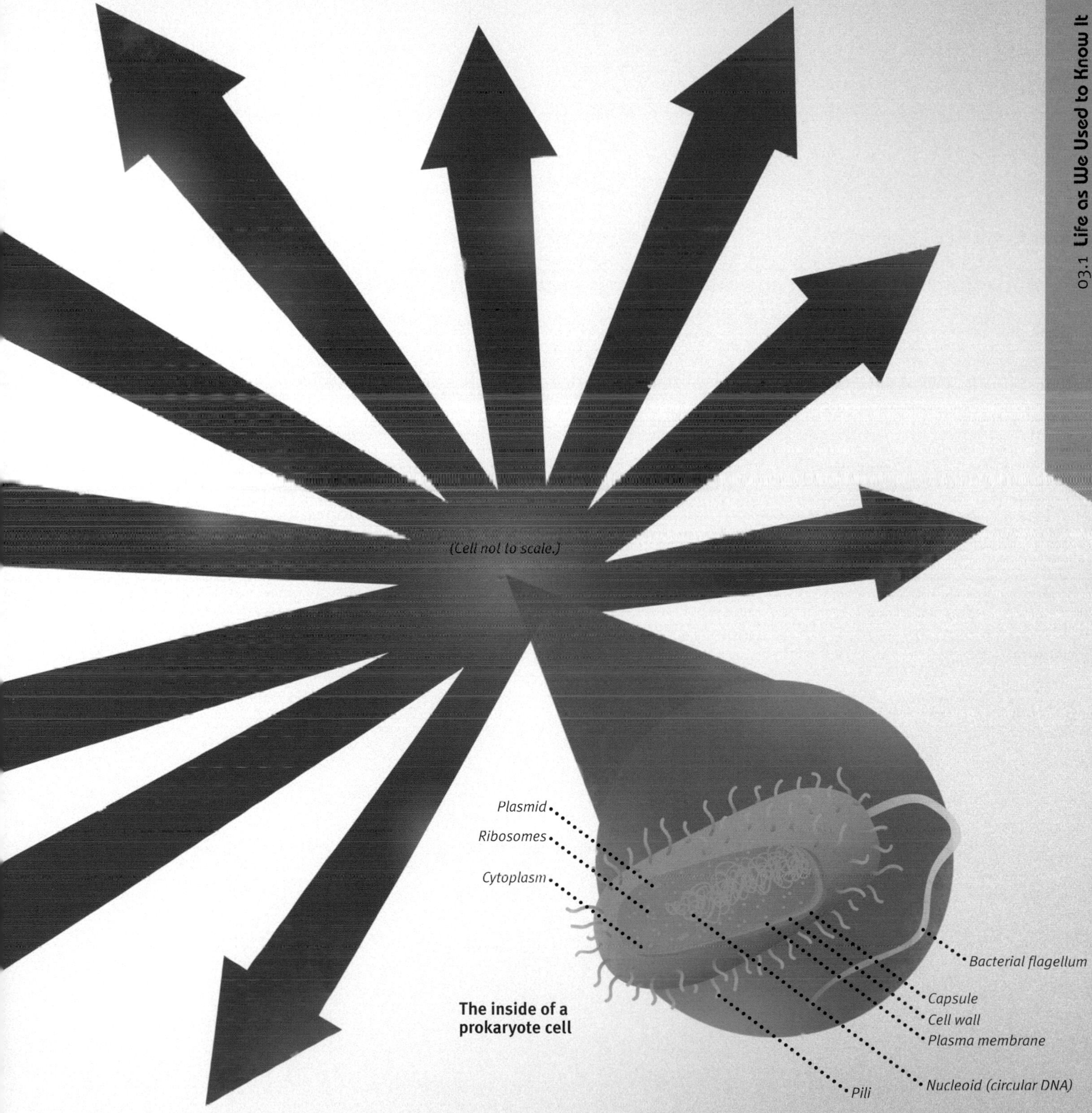

(Cell not to scale.)

Plasmid

Ribosomes

Cytoplasm

Bacterial flagellum

Capsule

Cell wall

Plasma membrane

**The inside of a
prokaryote cell**

Nucleoid (circular DNA)

Pili

And Then There Were Cells_

As you can see from this timeline, while it took nearly three billion years to go from **simple prokaryotes to multicellular life**, it took just a third of that time to go from the first multicellular life-forms to humans. Each successive step on the timeline is as significant as the previous one, but happens much, *much* quicker.

Let's concentrate on the main "jumps" that led to us—*Homo sapiens*.

1. Simple cells (prokaryotes)
The first living thing and the building block for everything since. Born in a primordial soupy broth.

2. Photosynthesis
Without this, the planet would not have developed its beautifully balanced environment.

3. Ozone layer
The formulation of this created a shield from the Sun's ultraviolet light and made the planet habitable. It is from this moment on that the planet suddenly ("suddenly" being a relative term) became populated by living things.

4. Death of the dinosaurs
With dinosaurs around, it is unlikely that humans would have come along.

5. Genus *Homo*
The first appearance of the genus *Homo* evolved out of *Australopithecus*—the final precursor before *Homo*. This is the last major change on human beings' evolutionary journey.

3.8 billion years of simple cells (prokaryotes)

3 billion years of photosynthesis

There are two types of primary cells: eurokaryotic and prokaryotic. Eurokaryotic cells have a nucleus. Animals, plants, and fungi are made up of eurokaryotic cells. Bacteria, which constitute 95 percent of all cells found in the body, are made of prokaryotic cells.

2 billion years of complex cells (eukaryotes)

1 billion years of multicellular life

600 million years of simple animals

570 million years of arthropods (ancestors of insects, arachnids, and crustaceans)

550 million years of complex animals

500 million years of fish and protoamphibians

475 million years of land plants

400 million years of insects and seeds

350 million years of amphibians

300 million years of reptiles

200 million years of mammals

150 million years of birds

130 million years of flowers

65 million years since the nonavian dinosaurs died out

2.5 million years since the appearance of the genus Homo

200,000 years since humans started looking like they do today

25,000 years since Neanderthals died out

03.3 Photosynthesis_

The process of photosynthesis—taking in carbon dioxide and converting it into oxygen—is vital to life on Earth.

To explain this process in plants, there is a complex equation:

$6CO_2 + 6H_2O$ **energy from sunlight produces** $C_6H_{12}O_6 + 6O_2$ ....

But in effect, it is actually quite straightforward:

Carbon dioxide + water + energy from sunlight produces sugar + oxygen

Photosynthesis is important because it is the only process by which food is produced from the Sun's energy. This leads directly to all the benefits that the plants provide us with—and without it, we would not be here.

Something to Think About . . .

Plants are only really concerned with the production of sugar in the process of photosynthesis. The oxygen that occurs as a result of this is, in fact, a waste product, which is why plants just release it into the air.

The energy for photosynthesis comes from light.

Plants conduct photosynthesis in specialized cells called chloroplasts.

Light energy

Oxygen

Carbon dioxide enters the leaves through tiny holes, or stomata.

Carbon dioxide

Water

The oxygen atoms from the water molecules form oxygen gas molecules.

Light energy is converted into chemical energy by chlorophyll—a pigment that energizes electrons using specific wavelengths of light. Chlorophyll is also what gives all plants their green colors.

$$C_6H_{12}O_6 + 6O_2$$

The Life Cycle of a Tree_

In addition to the vital role they play in producing oxygen for us to breathe, trees—and their wood—have other uses that are equally important to humans and animals. Trees are used for many of the basic requirements needed for a comfortable existence:

Warmth: Wood is a principal material used for making fires.

Cooking: Fires provide a method of cooking and heating water.

Shelter: Wood was once the main material for house building all over the world, and in many developing places it still is. However, since the invention of strong metals, wood plays a reduced part in the construction of houses. But even in countries where wood is not the main component, it is still used as part of a building's structure. Trees also play a vital role in animal habitats, providing a living environment for many animals, birds, and insects.

Transportation: Almost all early methods of transportation relied on wood, especially for covering the distances between landmasses across the oceans.

Furniture: Practically every house contains something made of wood, be it a chair, a table, or maybe just a fruit bowl.

Communication: The invention of the printing press in 1440 played an important part in enabling better communication around the world, but without paper, which is of course made from wood, it would have been impossible to spread the written word so well.

Something to Think About . . .

An acorn that falls to the ground has around a 1 in 10,000 chance of developing into a mature oak tree.

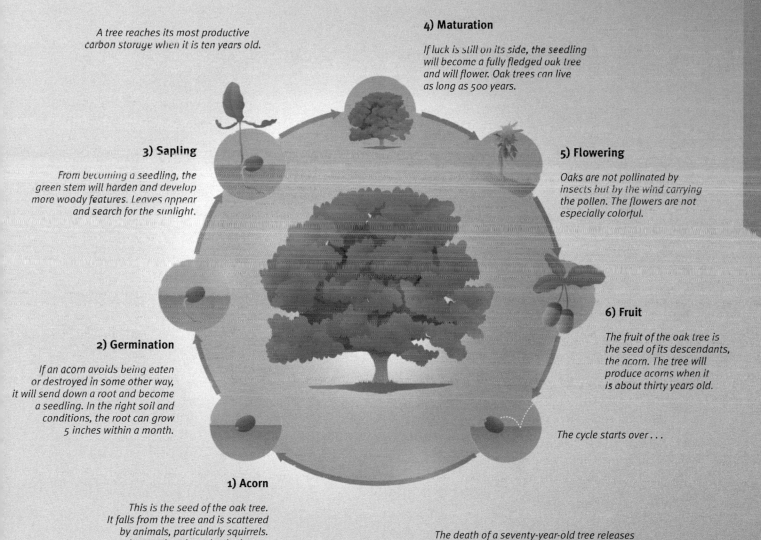

4) Maturation

If luck is still on its side, the seedling will become a fully fledged oak tree and will flower. Oak trees can live as long as 500 years.

A tree reaches its most productive carbon storage when it is ten years old.

3) Sapling

From becoming a seedling, the green stem will harden and develop more woody features. Leaves appear and search for the sunlight.

5) Flowering

Oaks are not pollinated by insects but by the wind carrying the pollen. The flowers are not especially colorful.

6) Fruit

The fruit of the oak tree is the seed of its descendants, the acorn. The tree will produce acorns when it is about thirty years old.

2) Germination

If an acorn avoids being eaten or destroyed in some other way, it will send down a root and become a seedling. In the right soil and conditions, the root can grow 5 inches within a month.

The cycle starts over . . .

1) Acorn

This is the seed of the oak tree. It falls from the tree and is scattered by animals, particularly squirrels. Acorns that the animals drop or don't get around to eating may then germinate.

The death of a seventy-year-old tree releases three tons of carbon back into the atmosphere.

73

03.5 The Kingdom of Insects_

Insects are an important part of the **planet's ecosystem,** and with over a million named and identified species, they outnumber all other groups of living creatures. Not only can they be found everywhere, but insects are often the only things that can survive in some of the **world's harshest environments**.

Because of their relative size, one main function of insects is to be at the bottom of the food chain, but it would be unfair to think of them simply as a **source of nutrition** for everything else. Insects play an essential role in allowing the flora to flourish by **pollinating** trees and flowers, aerating the soil, and helping dead animals and plants to decompose, thereby **introducing nutrients** into the soil. They also fertilize soil with their own waste and control each other's numbers for the eventual benefit of plant life.

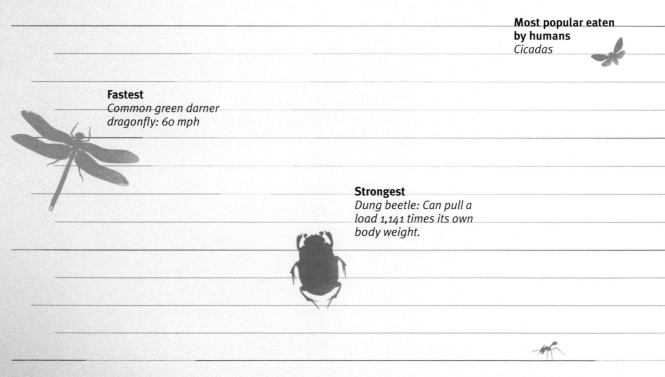

Most popular eaten by humans
Cicadas

Fastest
Common green darner dragonfly: 60 mph

Strongest
Dung beetle: Can pull a load 1,141 times its own body weight.

Most toxic venom
Pogonomyrmex ant

Something to Think About . . .

One urban myth states that humans swallow up to eight spiders a year in their sleep. No research has been carried out on this, but 60 percent of people think it is true.

Longest
Walking stick insect: 12 inches

Smallest
Fairy fly (a type of wasp): 0.007–0.15 inch

Heaviest
Giant weta (a type of cricket): 2.5 ounces

The Kingdom of Mammals_

Mammals were present on Earth during the age of the dinosaurs, but it was only after the dinosaurs became extinct that these **warm-blooded creatures**—from which human beings evolved—really began to diversify.

One of the main factors that led to this "branching out" was the disintegration of the supercontinent Pangaea during the **Mesozoic era,** which caused a diaspora of mammals and plants to flourish in different parts of the planet with different climates. This pollination of life around the world took about 65 million years, which may seem like a long time to us, but this is relatively short compared to the age of the planet.

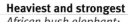

Heaviest and strongest
*African bush elephant:
11 tons*

Smallest
*Kitti's hog-nosed bat:
0.7 ounces*

It's a Fact . . .

The Bering land bridge was important in allowing animals that evolved in North America to travel to Asia. The bridge linked Alaska to what is now Siberia.

Something to Think About . . .

Alligators' jaws have an exceptionally strong closing force. However, the best way to avoid being eaten by an alligator is to hold its mouth shut—it has hardly any opening strength.

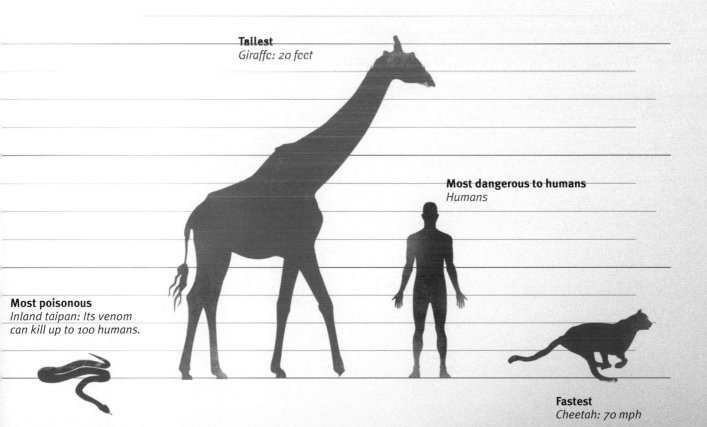

Tallest
Giraffe: 20 feet

Most dangerous to humans
Humans

Most poisonous
Inland taipan: Its venom can kill up to 100 humans.

Fastest
Cheetah: 70 mph

The Kingdom of the Sea_

Fish and most ocean-dwelling creatures have been on Earth since before the dinosaurs, and the **world's first vertebrates**—animals with backbones—were actually jawless fish. This type of fish was not particularly successful, and has left few descendants. This was a result of the limitations imposed by their inability to feed due to the lack of a hinged jaw. It is therefore no surprise that the fish that did develop a jaw superseded them in the fight for survival. This evolutionary step was vital—it enabled the fish to eat a much greater variety of food.

Fish are divided into three classes: **Agnatha** (jawless fish such as hagfish), **Chondrichthyes** (cartilaginous fish such as sharks), and **Osteichyes** (bony fish, which icludes most other fishes). It is from fish, which dominated in the Devonian period (416–357 million years ago), that land animals first evolved.

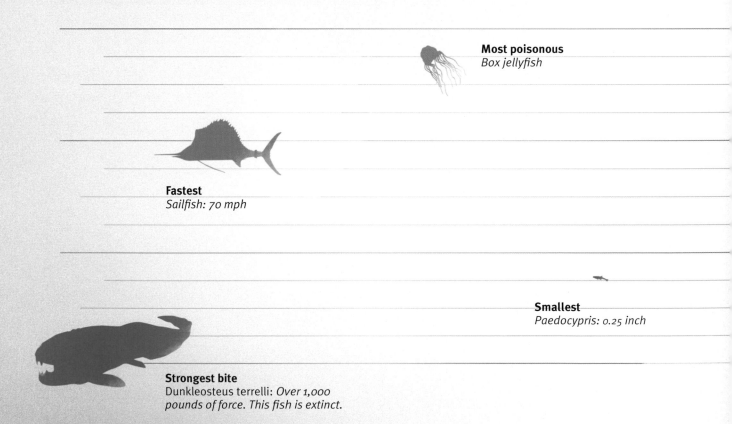

Most poisonous
Box jellyfish

Fastest
Sailfish: 70 mph

Smallest
Paedocypris: 0.25 inch

Strongest bite
Dunkleosteus terrelli: *Over 1,000 pounds of force. This fish is extinct.*

Something to Think About . . .

The number of scales a fish has stays the same throughout its life. It doesn't develop more as it grows; its scales just get bigger.

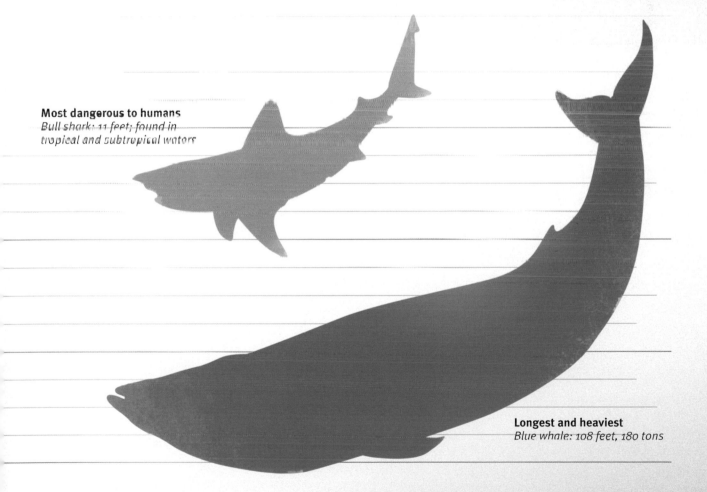

Most dangerous to humans
Bull shark: 11 feet; found in tropical and subtropical waters

Longest and heaviest
Blue whale: 108 feet, 180 tons

03.8 The Kingdom of Birds_

Birds are direct descendants of theropod dinosaurs, the best known of which is *Tyrannosaurus rex*.

The thing that makes birds different from most other vertebrates is their ability to fly. The adaptations that allow flight are an ultra-lightweight skeleton (thanks to hollow bones), exceptionally strong pectoralis muscles, and the aerodynamic shape of the wings.

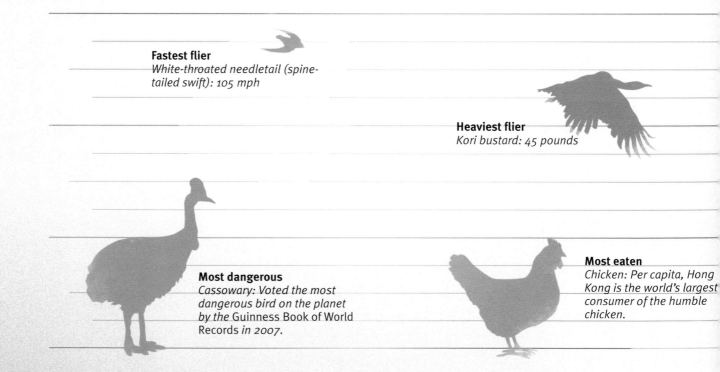

Fastest flier
White-throated needletail (spine-tailed swift): 105 mph

Heaviest flier
Kori bustard: 45 pounds

Most dangerous
Cassowary: Voted the most dangerous bird on the planet by the Guinness Book of World Records *in 2007.*

Most eaten
Chicken: Per capita, Hong Kong is the world's largest consumer of the humble chicken.

Something to Think About . . .

Flamingos are pink because of their food, which is rich in carotene—the same substance that gives carrots their color.

Biggest flier
Wandering albatross:
11-foot wingspan

Heaviest, tallest, and strongest
Ostrich: 10 feet, 350 pounds

Smallest
Bee hummingbird:
2 inches, 0.06 ounce

03.9 The Age of Dinosaurs_

When did dinosaurs rule the Earth . . . and for how long?

The first dinosaurs appeared during the **Triassic period**, 250–210 million years ago (mya), when Earth had just one supercontinent, Pangaea. Their peak, when they dominated the planet, was the **Jurassic period**, 210–150 mya. At this time, the continent was beginning to break up, and the **Cretaceous period** (150–65 mya) saw the distribution of the landmasses beginning to resemble those of today. Toward the end of this period, the most famous and fiercest dinosaur, *Tyrannosaurus rex*, ruled the roost—but was not the *biggest* dinosaur, contrary to popular myth. A sauropod known as Argentinosaurus—weighing in at 100 tons and reaching a height of 120 feet—takes the prize of being the biggest dinosaur found so far.

What was the gap between them and us? We—that is, *Homo sapiens*—appeared about 250,000 years ago.

Triassic period
250–210 mya
(Eoraptor, Coelophysis, Herrerasaurus)

Jurassic period
210–150 mya
(Brachiosaurus, Scelidosaurus, Dilophosauru

Something to Think About . . .

To date, more than 700 different species of dinosaurs have been discovered, identified, and named. However, paleontologists are certain that there are many more species (and the fossils they have left behind) still to be discovered.

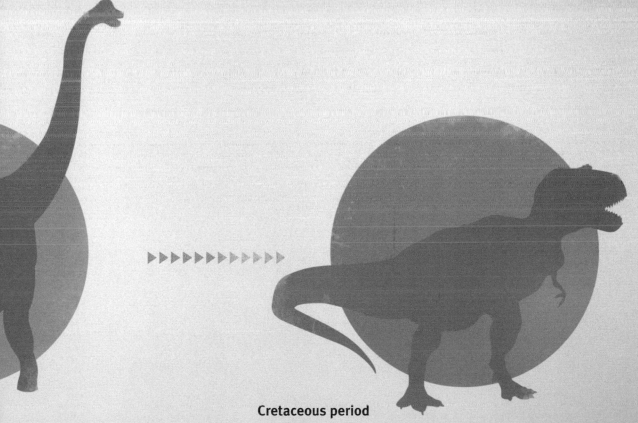

Cretaceous period
150–65 mya
(Tyrannosaurus, Ornithomimus, Triceratops)

03.10 **What Killed the Dinosaurs?**

The **K-T boundary** is the point on the prehistoric timeline that indicates when the dinosaurs disappeared. This boundary refers to the periods on either side of the line: **K** (Cretaceous) and **T** (Tertiary). Fossil records show the existence of dinosaurs on the K side of the boundary but not on the T side (providing we ignore birds, which are direct descendants of dinosaurs).

The ongoing scientific debate revolves not around the fact that Earth's climate changed dramatically and suddenly 65 million years ago (thus destroying the atmosphere and environment vital for dinosaur survival) but around the question of why the climate changed so drastically. What happened to Earth for everything to change *so* fast?

The most common and established theory to answer this question was proposed by Walter Alvarez and his team of geologists in 1980. Alvarez theorized that an asteroid hit Earth, instantly killing everything within a 300-mile radius and throwing a huge amount of debris up into the atmosphere. This debris quickly blocked out sunlight, causing the temperature to drop, and led to the rapid extinction of the dinosaurs and **75 percent of all living species** that inhabited the planet.

Something to Think About . . .

There are two reasons we want to know what happened to the dinosaurs. First, we're just interested—it is just this type of curiosity that has pushed mankind to great heights. Second, and probably more important, if something could wipe dinosaurs off the face of the planet, couldn't the same happen to us? If so, wouldn't it be good to know what that something is before it happens again?

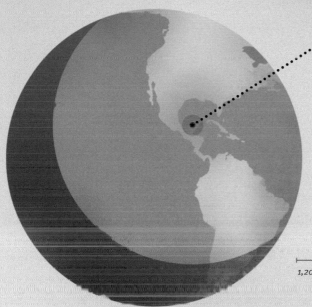

Dinosaur killer

When: 65 million years ago
Location: Chicxulub, Yucatán Peninsula, Mexico
Size of crater: 112 miles in diameter
Size of asteroid: 6 miles in diameter
Size of explosion (in energy): 2,000,000 times the biggest thermonuclear bomb, or 100 million megatons of TNT
Level of destruction: 75 percent of all species on Earth wiped out

1,200 miles

A comparative study of the impact of the asteroid that killed off the dinosaurs 65 million years ago and the 1945 Hiroshima bomb.

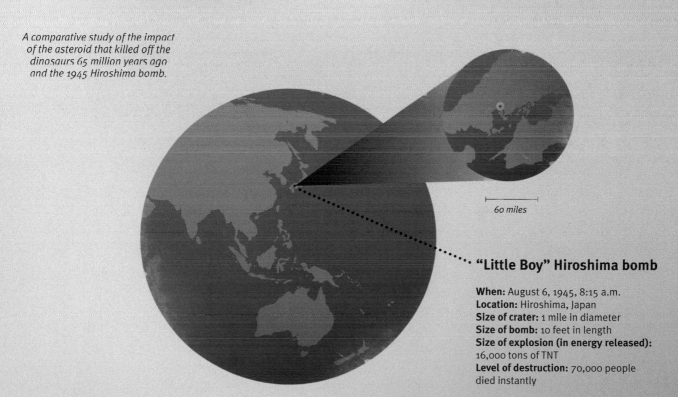

60 miles

"Little Boy" Hiroshima bomb

When: August 6, 1945, 8:15 a.m.
Location: Hiroshima, Japan
Size of crater: 1 mile in diameter
Size of bomb: 10 feet in length
Size of explosion (in energy released): 16,000 tons of TNT
Level of destruction: 70,000 people died instantly

85

The Food Chain_

The food chain is an easy way of looking at the movement and direction of food (which provides the energy needed to sustain life) from one animal to another within an ecosystem or habitat. The food chain is a vital part of an ecosystem and shows how the survival of one species is connected closely to the survival of others.

No matter what food chain we begin with, we always start with the **primary producer**—the lowest level on the chain (i.e., the first to be eaten). The position occupied on the chain is referred to as the **trophic level**. The primary producer is at level one.

For instance, in a food chain beginning with grass (primary producer), the next trophic level up would be the grasshopper—the **primary consumer**. The grasshopper is then eaten by a lizard, which is a **secondary consumer**. The lizard will then be eaten by a **tertiary consumer**, and so on. Many organisms and animals may assume different trophic levels on different food chains.

The balance of the planet's ecosystems depends on keeping all levels of these chains constantly supplied. If there is a shortfall at any level, there will be repercussions all the way up and down the chain. If there are not enough producers to supply the consumers, then the consumers will die off. If a consumer dies out, a producer may become too dominant and kill off its own producer, and so on.

Many food chains around the world are currently threatened by the destruction of animal habitats such as rain forests.

Something to Think About . . .

Those at the top of a food chain are called "apex predators." Humans are the most obvious example, but other apex predators include whales, tigers, and eagles.

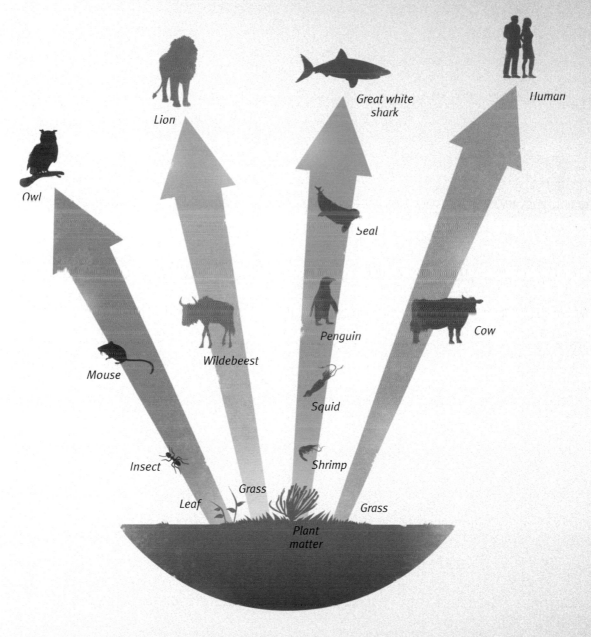

Owl

Lion

Great white
shark

Human

Seal

Mouse

Wildebeest

Penguin

Cow

Squid

Insect

Shrimp

Grass

Leaf

Grass

Plant
matter

*At each level, energy is passed on to the consumer, but there is always some energy lost.
In fact, less than 15 percent of energy is passed on at each level.*

The Life Span of Animals_

Daniel Defoe was probably the first writer to highlight that there are two certainties in life: death and taxes. What we don't know is when the former will come along.

All living things are born and then at some time later they die—but the gap in between these two events varies enormously from one organism to another. A mayfly, for example, can have a life span as short as thirty minutes, while the giant tortoise can expect to be around for more than 150 years. In the plant world, the bristlecone pine can live to an incredible 5,000 years.

Jeanne Calment has the **longest confirmed human life span**. She was born in Arles, France, on February 21, 1875, and died 122 years later on August 4, 1997.

Human male (in the developed world) 78 years *(12–15 y*

Human female (in the developed world) 83 years *(11–15 years)*

Something to Think About . . .

The plastic collar of a six-pack of soda cans will outlive us all—it won't break down for 400 years. This is, coincidentally, 399 years and 359 days longer than the actual six-pack is expected to last.

Elephant 70 years *(9 years)*

Mouse 4 years *(35 days for females, 60 days for males)*

Crocodile 45 years *(13 years for females, 16 years for males)*

Camel 50 years *(5 years)*

Queen bee 3 years *(5–7 days)*

Sheep 15 years *(6–8 months)*

Horse 40 years *(1–2 years)*

Tarantula 15 years *(2 years)*

Gerbil 5 years *(9–12 weeks)*

Kangaroo 9 years *(22 months)*

Dog 15 years *(6–12 months)*

Human male (Swaziland, Africa) 39.8 years *(lowest on the United Nations' list of life expectancy)*

Canary 24 years *(5 months)*

Cat 15–20 years *(7–12 months)*

Lion 35 years *(3–5 years)*

(Figures in parentheses indicate when the species becomes sexually active.)

Chapter 04.0 Humans_

The Evolution of Human Beings_

Like monkeys, apes, and even lemurs, human beings are classified as **primates**—the first of which appeared around 65 million years ago (mya), after the dinosaurs had died out and Earth's climate stabilized. While we could trace our evolution further back in history, this particular moment in time was really the start of our own distinct branch of evolution.

Fifteen million years after primates first appeared, the family Hominidae (great apes) evolved, but it was still another 10 million years before the emergence of the earliest known primate that displayed distinct elements of human beings. The proof of this is a fossil of *Ardipithecus ramidus* dating from around 4.5 mya that shows it to be predominantly bipedal (two-legged). *Ardipithecus ramidus* was followed 3–4 mya by *Australopithecus anamensis* and *Australopithecus afarensis*, both of which show signs of permanent bipedalism. The brain at this evolutionary step was still small, and facial features were still mainly apelike, but the teeth were gradually becoming smaller.

Something to Think About . . .

It is believed that toward the end of the late Pleistocene epoch, about 75,000 years ago, the number of *Homo sapiens sapiens* got as low as 1,000 breeding couples, and it is from this small group that we are all descended.

The Neanderthal was as strong, intelligent, and resourceful as *Homo sapiens*, but around 30,000 years ago they became extinct, while *Homo sapiens* flourished and eventually became *Homo sapiens sapiens*—that's us.

Homo erectus came next around 1.8 mya. The facial features are now closer to human than ape, body hair has greatly reduced, and brain size is about 75 percent that of a modern human's.

Fossil remains have been found of *Homo habilis*, along with primitive tools. Standing around 5 feet tall, *Homo habilis* had a brain cavity big enough to house an organ capable of primitive speech.

Over the next two million years, evolution began to speed up with three further species of *Australopithecus*: *A. africanus*, *A. robustus*, and then *A. boisei* around 1 mya. These overlap with the appearance of *Homo habilis* about 2.5 mya.

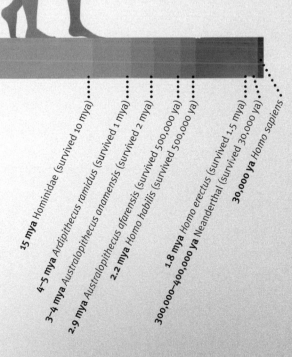

65 mya First primates (survived 50 mya)

15 mya Hominidae (survived 10 mya)

4–5 mya Ardipithecus ramidus (survived 1 mya)

3–4 mya Australopithecus anamensis (survived 1 mya)

2.9 mya Australopithecus afarensis (survived 2 mya)

2.2 mya Homo habilis (survived 500,000 ya)

1.8 mya Homo erectus (survived 500,000 ya)

300,000–400,000 ya Neanderthal (survived 1.5 mya)

30,000 ya Homo sapiens

04.2 Human Composition_

What is the recipe for a human?

Most people know that we're made mostly of water—on average, around 60 percent of our body weight. But where do we keep it, and why don't we drip everywhere?

Most of it is **intracellular fluid**, meaning that it is contained within the living cells of the body. Our blood represents only about 5 percent of our total body weight. Of the remaining 40 percent of our body weight, around 18 percent is **fat**, 15 percent is **protein**, and the other 7 percent is **minerals**, mainly in the form of **bone**.

Something to Think About . . .

The human body is a miracle, but we often take it for granted. In order for it to carry out the simplest (or what we assume are simple) instructions, our brain must orchestrate and utilize many different muscles—as well as express many differing emotions—at the same time. Reading this sentence, for example, involves the complex movement of many eye muscles straining together, the coordination of the relevant brain centers in interpreting the meaning of the words, and then deciphering how it makes you feel.

Average time between blinks of the eyes:
2.8 seconds

Potassium 0.35%

Phosphorus 1.1%

Calcium 2%

Nitrogen 3%

Carbon 18%

Total number of human taste buds:
10,000

Oxygen 65%

There are 2.5 trillion red blood cells in your body
at any moment. Your body creates 2.5 million
new red blood cells per second.

Number of receptor cells in your nose:
12 million (a dog has 1 billion!)

Hydrogen 10%

Sulfur 0.25%

Chlorine 0.15%

Sodium 0.15%

**Magnesium, iron, manganese,
copper, iodine, cobalt, zinc**
traces

DNA_

Deoxyribonucleic acid, or DNA as most of us call it, holds all the **genetic information** of a living thing. Although it was first discovered by Swiss scientist Friedrich Miescher in 1871, it was an American, James D. Watson, and a Briton, Francis Crick, who in 1953 first correctly modeled the **double-helix** structure that makes up what we recognize as DNA.

The DNA that we are made up of individually is inherited from our parents, and it is the information held in this DNA that gives us characteristics of both parents. The mix will always vary, which is why siblings do not look the same, except in the case of identical twins who develop from the same egg—and therefore have the exact same combination of **chromosomes**.

Among all human beings, 99.9 percent of our DNA is identical. However, the 0.1 percent difference is enough to distinguish one person's look, features, and personality from another's—this is what makes you *you*. It is this 0.1 percent that has allowed **genetic fingerprinting** to be used by police to aid in their investigations.

Something to Think About . . .

Because everything on the planet originates from the same place, most likely the big bang, we share elements of our DNA with everything else. For instance, 60 percent of our DNA is the same as a banana's.

04.4 The Brain_

Our brain is the center of everything we are. It holds our memories, controls all our bodily functions, and perhaps most importantly, allows us to think. When humans learned to use fire and started cooking meat, the amount of blood used to digest food was reduced. This excess blood allowed the brain to grow in size, evolve, and develop—thereby enabling us to move ahead of the pack.

The brain comprises three main parts: the **cerebral cortex**, the **cerebellum**, and the **brain stem**. The cerebral cortex is further split into four lobes: **frontal**, **parietal**, **temporal**, and **occipital**. These lobes are connected by, and made up of, **neurons** and **glia**. The neurons do the grunt work of sending electric signals around the body, while the glia acts as a bodyguard for the neurons, protecting and nourishing them.

Much of the research into the brain, and identifying which parts are responsible for which function, is based on monitoring people's behavior when certain parts of the brain are injured, or even removed.

Something to Think About . . .

The brain weighs around 3 pounds, which, as a percentage of body weight, makes it the biggest brain of any animal. There are 100 billion neurons in the brain. It is 78 percent water, 11 percent lipids, 8 percent protein, 1 percent carbohydrate, and 2 percent other stuff. It is difficult to calculate the storage space in the brain, but some estimates have it as high as 1,000 terabytes.

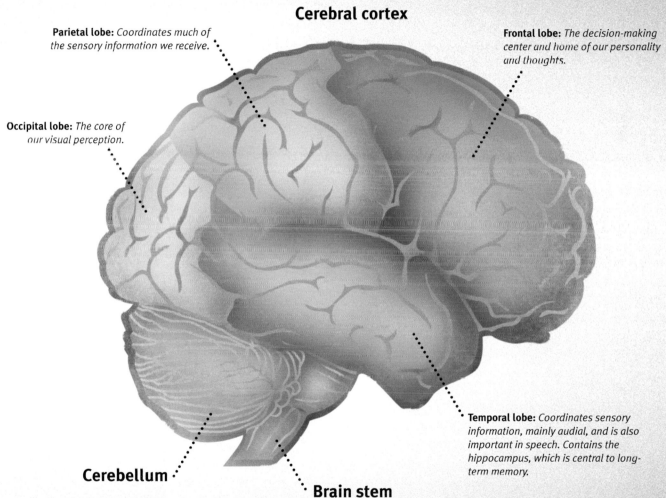

Cerebral cortex

Parietal lobe: *Coordinates much of the sensory information we receive.*

Frontal lobe: *The decision-making center and home of our personality and thoughts.*

Occipital lobe: *The core of our visual perception.*

Temporal lobe: *Coordinates sensory information, mainly audial, and is also important in speech. Contains the hippocampus, which is central to long-term memory.*

Cerebellum

Receives information regarding movement, refines it, and sends the signals to the relevant parts of the body. Less understood is the part it plays in thought processes.

Brain stem

Vital in that it connects the brain to the rest of the body. Lower half is the medulla oblongata, which regulates unconscious activity such as breathing and heartbeat.

Total number of neurons in the brain: 100 billion

04.5 Skeleton and Muscles_

While research into the human brain is still in its infancy, our knowledge of the body is incredibly advanced.

An adult human has **206 bones,** and together these form the **skeleton**, around which everything else in the human body is organized. Our vital organs are held within the protective confines of the **rib cage**, our brain is protected by the **skull,** and we are covered in a protective layer, the outermost part of which is the **skin**.

We have between 600 and 800 muscles in our body, and these fall into three types: **skeletal, smooth,** and **cardiac**. Skeletal muscles are connected to our bones and are used for motion. We consciously control these actions. Smooth muscles make up the walls of organs such as the bladder and stomach. These muscles operate automatically without us having to instruct them. Finally there is the cardiac muscle, the **heart**. This is the only muscle that never rests, and its job is to pump blood around the body.

Something to Think About . . .

Babies have over 300 bones and much more cartilage than adults. As they mature, the cartilage ossifies into bone, and thus some of their bones are fused, resulting in the 206 bones present in the body of a fully mature adult.

Main muscles and bones of the body

Frontalis · **Skull**

Orbicularis oris *(circular muscle of the eyelids)* · · · · · · · · · · · **Frontal bone** *(forehead)*

· · · · · · · · **Zygoma** *(cheekbone)*

· · · · · · · · · **Maxilla** *(upper jawbone)*

Sternocleidomastoids *(neck)* · · · · · · · · · · ·

Trapezius *(back, spine support)* · · · · · · · · · · · · ·

Deltoids *(triangular shoulder muscles)* · · · · · · · · · · · · · · **Clavicle** *(collarbone)*

Pectorals *(chest)* · · · · · · · · · · · · · ·

Heart · · · · · · · · · · · · · · · · ·

Triceps *(back, upper arms)* · · · · · · · · · · · **Humerus** *(Upper arm)*

Biceps *(arm muscle with two points of attachment)* · · · · · · · · · ·

Latissimus dorsi *(back muscle)* · · · · · · · · · · · · ·

Rectus abdominus *(stomach)* · · · · · · · · · · · · · · · **Ulna** *(lesser forearm bone)*

· · · · · · · · · · · · · **Radius** *(main forearm bone)*

· · · · · · · · · · · · **Carpals** *(wrist bones)*

· · · · · · · · · · · · **Illum, pubis, ischium** *(pelvic bones)*

Gluteus maximus *(buttocks)* · · · · · · · · · · · · · · ·

Sartorius *(thigh, longest muscle in the body)* ·

Hamstrings *(back of thigh)* · · · · · · · · · · · · ·

Quadriceps *(front of thigh)* · · · · · · · · · · · · · · **Femur** *(thighbone)*

· · · · · · · · · · · **Patella** *(kneecap)*

· · · · · · · · · · · **Tibia** *(main shinbone)*

Gastrocnemius *(two calf muscles)* · · · · · · · · · · · · **Fibula** *(calf bone)*

Achilles tendon *(back, attaches calf to heel)* · · · · · · · · · · · ·

· · · · · · · · · **Tarsals** *(anklebones)*

· · · · · · · **Metatarsals** *(foot bones)*

· · · · · · **Phalanges** *(toe bones)*

· · · · · **Calcaneus** *(heel)*

The Senses_

The importance of the head, skull, and brain is demonstrated by the fact that **four of the five senses** are housed and operated solely within that area. Touch is the odd one out but is still controlled by the brain, which processes the pressure signals that come from all over the body.

Humans are predominantly visual creatures. We are able to see things because **light enters the eye** and is focused onto the **retina** at the back of the eyeball. The cells in the retina convert this information into **electrical signals,** which are sent to the brain to interpret. Different cells in the retina deal with color and brightness.

Sound waves make the **eardrum** vibrate. These vibrations are passed on to the cochlea, within which are hair cells that generate a nerve impulse that is sent to the brain.

Taste begins when the taste buds, mainly on the tongue, are stimulated. There are five **receptors** that can detect **sweet, sour, bitter, salty,** and **umami.** Umami is a savory taste that was identified only in 1908 due to it being the most subtle of the five tastes. Indeed, many people do not even realize it exists.

Smell is closely related to taste and each can be affected by the loss of the other. It is triggered by the stimulation of **olfactory receptors** in the nose. There are many more smell receptors than there are taste receptors.

We perceive **touch** through the **receptors on our skin,** including the tiny hairs with which it is covered. The receptors vary in sensitivity depending on where they are on the body; for example, the palm of your hand is more sensitive to touch than the back of your hand.

Something to Think About . . .

We all have a blind spot where the optic nerve passes through the retina. Cover your left eye and look at the O from about 8 inches from the page. Slowly move away and the X will disappear.

O   X

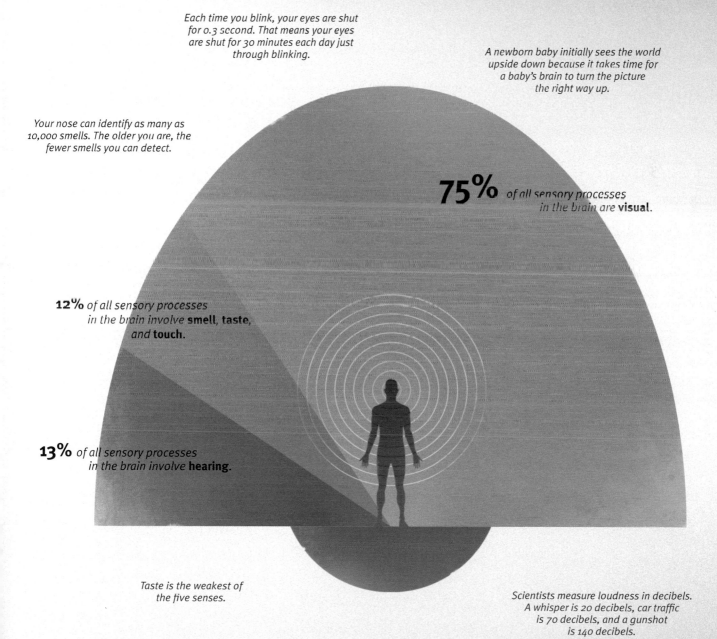

Each time you blink, your eyes are shut for 0.3 second. That means your eyes are shut for 30 minutes each day just through blinking.

A newborn baby initially sees the world upside down because it takes time for a baby's brain to turn the picture the right way up.

Your nose can identify as many as 10,000 smells. The older you are, the fewer smells you can detect.

75% *of all sensory processes in the brain are* **visual**.

12% *of all sensory processes in the brain involve* **smell, taste, and touch**.

13% *of all sensory processes in the brain involve* **hearing**.

Taste is the weakest of the five senses.

Scientists measure loudness in decibels. A whisper is 20 decibels, car traffic is 70 decibels, and a gunshot is 140 decibels.

Where Your Organs Are_

In the trunk of the human body, protected by the rib cage, are the **main organs**—everything but the brain. The most important of these organs is the **heart**, as it is this engine that pumps vital, **oxygen-enriched blood** all around the body and makes everything else work.

The oxygen carried in the blood is first processed by the **lungs**. Fresh oxygen is inhaled by breathing, which causes our lungs to expand. The oxygen in this air binds to the **hemoglobin** in the red blood cells, which then release their carbon dioxide. This carbon dioxide is expelled as the lungs contract.

The **kidneys** play an important role in keeping the blood clean. They process about 36 gallons of blood every day. The waste products and excess fluids are expelled as urine via the bladder.

The **liver** has many functions, the main one of which is the production of bile to help **food digestion**. It also helps keep the blood clean by disposing of worn-out red blood cells.

The **intestine**, split into the small and large intestines, processes food and extracts the protein, fats, carbohydrates, and vitamins. The small intestine is about 20 feet long, while the large intestine is only 5 feet long.

Something to Think About . . .

Our breathing happens subconsciously, but a dolphin has to make a conscious decision to take each breath.

Brain
Controls your body and mind.

Lungs

Heart
Circulates blood throughout body.

Liver
Breaks down toxins into less-poisonous compounds and creates proteins and amino acids.

Gallbladder
Stores bile for digestion.

Kidney
Makes urine from waste products and excess water in blood.

Large intestine
Converts food products into feces.

Appendix
Its function is unknown.

Lungs
Mixes blood with oxygen, disposes of used air and carbon dioxide.

Stomach
Receives food, stores it, then empties it into the duodenum.

Spleen
Filters, stores, and cleans blood.

Pancreas
Secretes digestive enzymes to control blood-sugar levels.

Kidney

Small intestine
Chemically digests food and helps absorb nutrients into bloodstream.

Bladder
Stores urine.

Skin
Protects body from infection, damage, and drying out.

04.8 The Cycle of Life_

The primary purpose of all living things is to guarantee the continuation of their species. We do this by **sexual reproduction**.

Sexual reproduction is the combination, or joining together, of **gametes**. In humans this is a **sperm** (from the male) and an **egg** (from the female). Together they create a new cell called a **zygote**.

Each gamete contains one set of **chromosomes**, while the new cell, the zygote, contains two sets—one from each parent. It is in these chromosomes that the genetic material from the parents is passed on to the infant.

The male reproductive system is made up of two parts: the **penis and the testicles**. The latter produces the **sperm**, while the former delivers it. Sperm does not survive for long, so men have to produce them constantly.

The female reproductive system comprises the **vagina and uterus**, as well as the **ovaries**. The ovaries produce the egg, and it is in the uterus that the sperm and egg combine.

Something to Think About . . .

Before sexual reproduction, cells just made copies of themselves. This meant that evolution only occurred when mistakes in the copying process were made. Sexual reproduction was a vital factor in speeding up evolution.

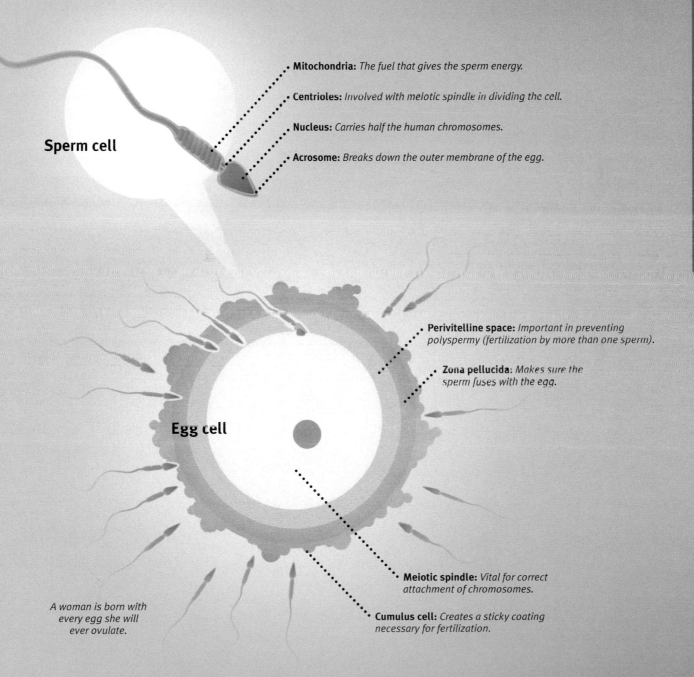

Sperm cell

Mitochondria: *The fuel that gives the sperm energy.*

Centrioles: *Involved with meiotic spindle in dividing the cell.*

Nucleus: *Carries half the human chromosomes.*

Acrosome: *Breaks down the outer membrane of the egg.*

Egg cell

Perivitelline space: *Important in preventing polyspermy (fertilization by more than one sperm).*

Zona pellucida: *Makes sure the sperm fuses with the egg.*

Meiotic spindle: *Vital for correct attachment of chromosomes.*

Cumulus cell: *Creates a sticky coating necessary for fertilization.*

A woman is born with every egg she will ever ovulate.

How the Body Works_

As humans evolved and we moved from a hunter-gatherer existence to a more sedentary lifestyle, it became necessary for us to be able to digest a wider variety and larger amount of food. Our digestive system evolved hand in hand with this need.

The first stage in the **digestive system** is the teeth, and these have changed quite remarkably over time. As our ability to cut food and cook it has improved, so have our teeth, helping the stomach to digest smaller and more manageable pieces of food.

The biggest single leap in the evolution of our digestive system was the discovery of **fire** as a method of cooking meat and vegetables. This process made it much easier for our stomachs to extract the **proteins** from the meat and gave humans access to nutrients in plants that were impossible to digest without cooking.

There are many systems that control the body. They are:

1. **The respiratory system** (regulates breathing)
2. **The cardiovascular system** (regulates blood flow)
3. **The digestive system** (regulates the processing of food)
4. **The endocrine system** (regulates the body's hormones)
5. **The immune system** (regulates the body's protective defenses)
6. **The reproductive system** (regulates sperm/egg production and fertilization)
7. **The excretory system** (regulates waste production)
8. **The nervous system** (regulates neurons)

Something to Think About . . .

While controlling fire was vital in cooking, it was also important in allowing human activity to extend beyond the hours of daylight. Our lives were no longer ruled by the Sun.

Mouth
Food enters here and is chewed to aid digestion.

Throat
Swallowing, a conscious decision, moves the food into the throat.

Esophagus
The link to the stomach. The connection is closed off by the lower esophageal sphincter. As food approaches, the sphincter relaxes to let the food in.

Stomach
Once the food is here, the work really begins. The food is mixed with digestive juices. When this process is complete, the stomach releases the digested food into the intestine.

Small intestine
This is where nutrients, fats, and carbohydrates are extracted into juices and passed to the pancreas and liver, while the remainder moves on to the large intestine.

Large intestine
Where final digestion occurs and the remaining bits of useful nutrients are extracted.

What is left after this is pushed into the colon and out past the final sphincter, the anus, as feces.

Throughout this system, our body produces digestive juices to help break down the food into nutrients, starting with saliva in the mouth, followed by bile from the liver.

The Development of Speech_

All animals communicate, but humans have—by far—the most sophisticated level of communication, and this is one more factor that has helped us get ahead of the pack.

Our earliest level of communication, during the time of the great apes 14 million years ago (mya), was at the same level as modern apes. The first development that allowed us to speak was the switch to **bipedalism**. This changed the position of the skull, making a variety of sounds possible.

Around the time of *Homo ergaster* (2.5 mya) and *Homo heidelbergenis* (600,000 years ago), it is thought that mothers developed a kind of "baby talk" to comfort their children, and this was the first properly vocalized human speech.

The fossil evidence of **advanced tools** that were produced using more than one substance or material is cited as proof of the further development of language and speech. The reasoning behind this is that, in order to pass on the knowledge of those tools' construction, there must have been some verbal communication.

One of the biggest leaps in the development of language was the ability to refer to things not in the immediate vicinity, either by time or place. While the teaching of toolmaking techniques was important, it is this function both of thought—and of vocalizing this thought—which brought our language skills to where we are today.

Taumatawhakatangihangak

Something to Think About . . .

The **Wernicke's area** (toward the back) and the **Broca's area** (near the front) are the two areas of the brain that control speech: the Wernicke's area decides what we want to say; the Broca's area sends the impulse to the muscles to produce the sounds.

The longest words in several languages

French (meaning "unconstitutionally"; 25 letters)
Anticonstitutionnellement

German (a German law regarding the labeling of beef; 63 letters)
...dfleischetikettierungsüberwachungsaufgabenübertragungsgesetz

Pneumonoultramicroscopicsilicovolcanokoniosis
English (a type of lung disease; 45 letters)

Nghiêng
Vietnomese (meaning "inclined"; 7 letters)

וניתידפולקיצנאלשכו
Hebrew (meaning "and when to our encyclopedias"; 19 letters)

ワノオトヒメノモトコイノキリハズ
Japanese (a type of seaweed; 21 letters)

TaumatawhakatangihangakoauauotamateaturipukakapikimaungahoronukupokaiwhenuakItanatahu
Maori (a Maori place-name—the longest place-name in the world; 85 letters)

Dampskipsundervannsstyrkeprøvemaskinerikonstruksjonsvanskeligheter
Norwegian (meaning "steamship-underwater-strength-test-machinery-construction-difficulties"; 66 letters)

Electroencefalografistas
Spanish (a technician who uses an electroencephalograph; 24 letters)

Precipitevolissimevolmente
Italian (to precipitate, to be hasty, sudden and rash; 26 letters)

It's a Fact . . .

Hippopotomonstrosesquipedaliophobia (35 letters) is the fear of long words.

Memory_

If we are who we are because of all the things we experience, then memory is fundamental to what makes us who we *are*. If we had no memory, we would be reborn every second.

The process of remembering has **three** basic stages: **registering**, **storing**, and **retrieving**. It is generally felt that we have two main areas of storage: short-term and long-term.

When we register an event, a fact, or even just a person's name, **neurons** are stimulated in our brain by the messages received through our senses. When we remember that event, these same neurons are activated in the same way, and the memory is **recalled**. The simplest analogy to remember this process is that of the oldest system used in computers, the punch card.

The difference between **long-term** and **short-term memory** is that for the latter the holes are not punched permanently, and it is only by repetition that the holes are retained and moved into the long-term space. The classic example often cited is a phone number. When we are told a number by a friend, we can retain that number in our short-term memory just long enough to dial it, but unless we repeat it several times, it will disappear from our memory.

Something to Think About . . .

Chunking is a simple way to help remember things—especially numbers. We do this quite naturally with phone numbers when we split them into chunks in our head. The optimum chunk size is three digits.

How human memory works

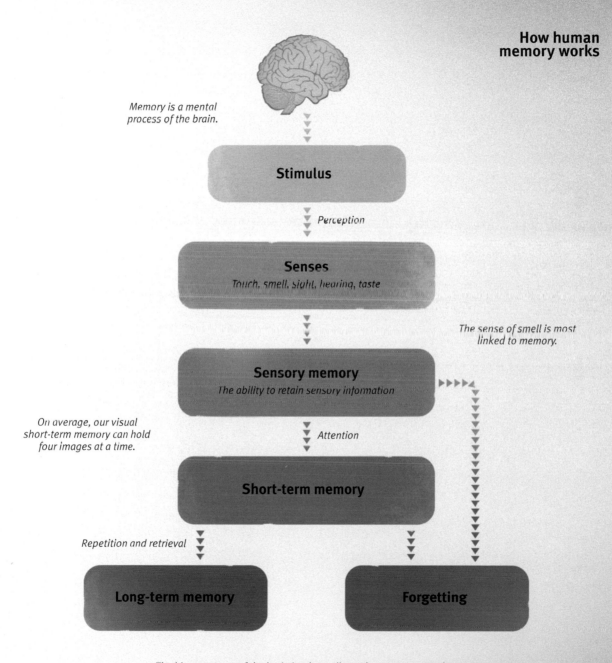

Memory is a mental process of the brain.

Stimulus

Perception

Senses
Touch, smell, sight, hearing, taste

The sense of smell is most linked to memory.

Sensory memory
The ability to retain sensory information

On average, our visual short-term memory can hold four images at a time.

Attention

Short-term memory

Repetition and retrieval

Long-term memory

Forgetting

The hippocampus of the brain is where all our short-term memories are formed and stored. When someone tells you a telephone number, your memory of the number goes directly to the hippocampus.

113

From Fertilization to Birth_

This timeline details the growth, size, and development of a baby in a womb.

Week 1
Fertilization and **cell division.**
The embryo is the size of the period at the end of this sentence.

Week 2
Size of a drawing pin
150 cells
Three layers: **endoderm** (becomes the respiratory and digestive systems), **mesoderm** (bones, circulatory system), **ectoderm** (brain, nervous system, hair, skin, and nails)

Week 4
Size of a grain of rice
0.2 inch
Embryo no longer looks like an egg. Buds for arms and legs appear.

Weeks 6–8
Size of a baked bean
0.3–0.8 inch/0.05–0.07 ounce
Eyes and ears begin to form as small cavities in the head. Brain cells and lungs are developing rapidly, reflexes are evident, and mouth can be opened. Bone forms, all vital organs are present.

Week 9
Size of a golf ball
2 inches/0.3 ounce
Mouth can open, eyes are fully formed, heart is beating at 150 beats per minute.

Week 11
Size of a credit card
3.3 inches/1 ounce
Vital organs can now function. Fetus can swallow.

Week 12
Size of a cell phone
4 inches/1.5 ounces
Facial muscles work.

Weeks 13–18
Size of a dollar bill
4.75–7.75 inches/2.25–4.75 ounces
Most body parts and organs are formed and in place. Heart beats twice as fast as mother's. Baby can hear, but can't interpret the sounds.

Weeks 19–20
Size of a soccer ball
8.25–9 inches/9.75–12.25 ounces
Milk teeth begin to form. A waxy coating, vernix,

Week 22
Size of a basketball
10.25 inches/16.75 ounces
White blood cells, which fight illness, are produced for the first time. Skin is still transparent.

Weeks 23–6
11–12.5 inches/19.5–26 ounces
First lines of fingerprints appear. Hearing system is now complete. Bones are hardening, baby sucks thumb, and can cry.

Weeks 27–30
13.75–14.5 inches/2–3 pounds
Eyes can open. If male, testes descend. Music heard now will be remembered after birth. Baby now fills all the available space in the womb.

Weeks 31–35
Size of a bowling pin
15.75–17.75 inches/3.75–5 pounds
Vernix and lanugo start to disappear. Baby practices breathing. Hair appears on head.

Week 38
19.5 inches/7 pounds
Lungs are ready for the world of air.

Birth

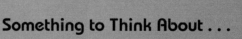

Something to Think About . . .

Lanugo is the name of a fine, downy hair that grows on a fetus. It helps regulate temperature and disappears before birth. Some animals, such as elephants, are born still covered with it.

Chapter 05.0 **Environment & Society_**

Population Growth_

All around the world, the growth of cities has followed the **mechanization** of **agriculture** and **farming**. As the demand for workers to bring in the food decreased, people were forced to move to the cities to find work.

In the first instance, cities drew workers from farms to work in factories, but as we have become more sophisticated in the way we produce things, the cities have become less important as **manufacturing** centers. In countries that are still developing, their major cities are still growing and producing things. In countries that we describe as "developed," the cities are full of **service industries** where nothing is actually made, but rather where it is sold or marketed.

As the populations in these **large cities** grow, there are two choices in how to accommodate them: they can either build up or build out, or even both. Thus these massive **metropolises** swallow up the towns and villages on their periphery.

What most major cities have in common is how they gained their status. In almost all cases, they are near water, either on the coast or a major river. Due to the ease of transportation afforded by waterways (rivers, ports, coasts), it is vital to a city's growth to have access to water nearby.

Something to Think About . . .

In England, the traditional way that a city is recognized is by the presence of a cathedral. Thus, relatively small places can be "cities," while some larger settlements remain as "towns."

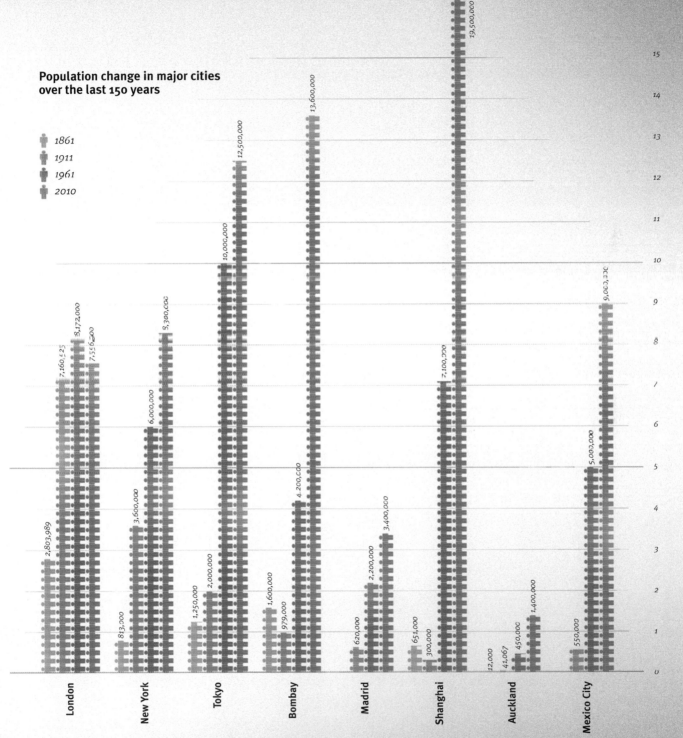

**Population change in major cities
over the last 150 years**

1861
1911
1961
2010

London
- 2,803,989
- 7,160,525
- 8,172,000
- 7,556,900

New York
- 813,000
- 3,500,000
- 6,000,000
- 8,300,000

Tokyo
- 1,250,000
- 2,000,000
- 10,000,000
- 12,500,000

Bombay
- 1,600,000
- 979,000
- 4,200,000
- 13,600,000

Madrid
- 620,000
- 2,200,000
- 3,400,000

Shanghai
- 651,000
- 300,000
- 7,100,000
- 19,500,000

Auckland
- 12,000
- 41,067
- 450,000
- 1,400,000

Mexico City
- 550,000
- 5,000,000
- 9,100,000

Total population

Staple Food Production_

With a global population quickly approaching **seven billion**, the big problem is how to feed everyone. Modern farming techniques have enabled us to grow larger quantities in increasingly smaller areas, but it is always going to be a massive task. According to the United Nations, almost one billion people do not have enough to eat. At the same time, even optimistic figures suggest that, globally, 20 percent of food is wasted. It does not take much imagination to see that we could feed everyone.

In all societies, certain foods are referred to as **staples**. These are generally cheap and readily available sources of nutrients, and will make up a major part of the regular diet, especially in poorer countries. Production of these staples is monopolized by a few countries around the globe. It is often cited that 80 percent of the world's food is produced by only 20 percent of the world.

Something to Think About . . .

Nearly 400,000,000 tons of rice are eaten each year around the world—the equivalent to four trillion 3.5-ounce servings.

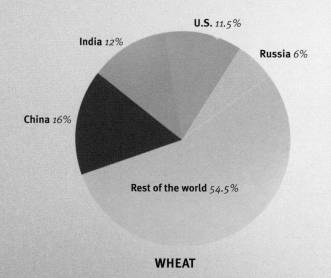

U.S. *11.5%*

India *12%*

Russia *6%*

China *16%*

Rest of the world *54.5%*

WHEAT

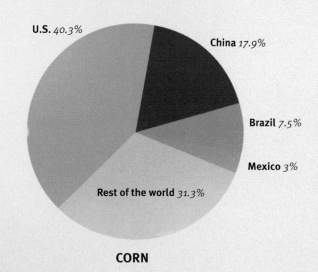

U.S. *40.3%*

China *17.9%*

Brazil *7.5%*

Mexico *3%*

Rest of the world *31.3%*

CORN

Production of staple foods by country of origin

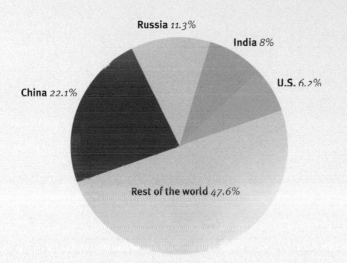

Russia *11.3%*

India *8%*

China *22.1%*

U.S. *6.2%*

Rest of the world *47.6%*

POTATOES

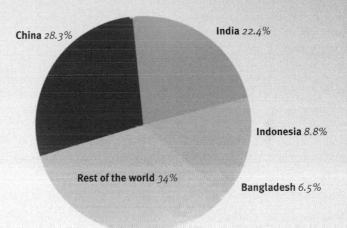

China *28.3%*

India *22.4%*

Indonesia *8.8%*

Rest of the world *34%*

Bangladesh *6.5%*

RICE

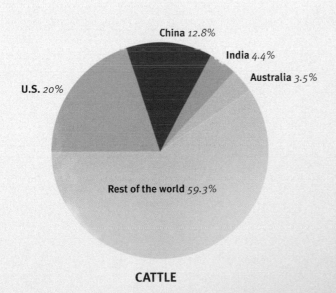

China *12.8%*

India *4.4%*

Australia *3.5%*

U.S. *20%*

Rest of the world *59.3%*

CATTLE

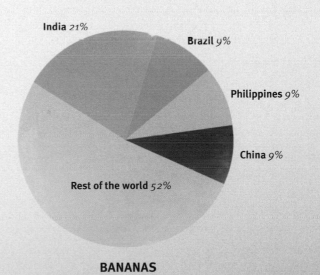

India *21%*

Brazil *9%*

Philippines *9%*

China *9%*

Rest of the world *52%*

BANANAS

05.3 The Science of Art_

Art began about 30,000 years ago with **cave drawings**. These depict what early humans saw in the immediate environment, which is why animals are predominant in the cave drawings.

In 1993 the British conceptual artist Damien Hirst exhibited *Mother and Child Divided*. The piece consists of four tanks of formaldehyde. Two of the tanks each contain half a cow, the other two each contain half a calf.

Art has traveled a long way, but has never moved.

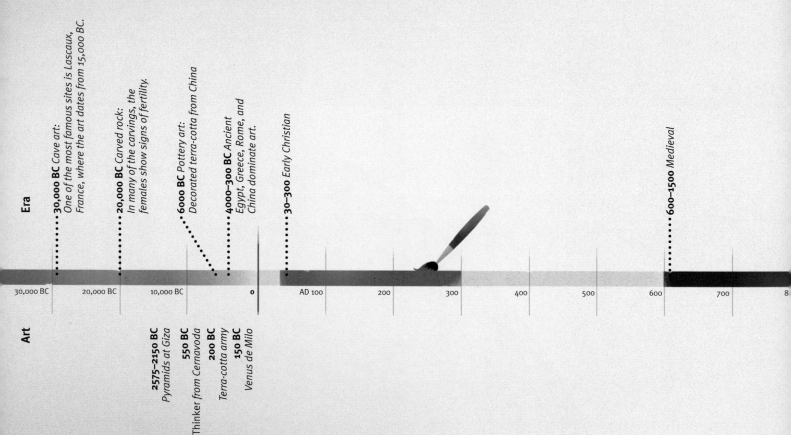

Era

30,000 BC *Cave art:*
One of the most famous sites is Lascaux,
France, where the art dates from 15,000 BC.

20,000 BC *Carved rock:*
In many of the carvings, the
females show signs of fertility.

6000 BC *Pottery art:*
Decorated terra-cotta from China

4000–300 BC *Ancient*
Egypt, Greece, Rome, and
China dominate art.

30–300 *Early Christian*

600–1500 *Medieval*

| 30,000 BC | 20,000 BC | 10,000 BC | 0 | AD 100 | 200 | 300 | 400 | 500 | 600 | 700 | 8 |

Art

2575–2150 BC
Pyramids at Giza

550 BC
Thinker from Cernavoda

200 BC
Terra-cotta army

150 BC
Venus de Milo

**A timeline detailing some of art's
greatest achievements and eras**

Something to Think About . . .

French artist Henri Matisse was a leading figure in modern art at the beginning of the twentieth century. However, in 1961 one of his works, *Le Bateau*, was hung upside down in the Museum of Modern Art in New York. Visitors to the museum did not notice this mistake despite the exhibit's popularity. It was finally hung the right way up after forty-seven days.

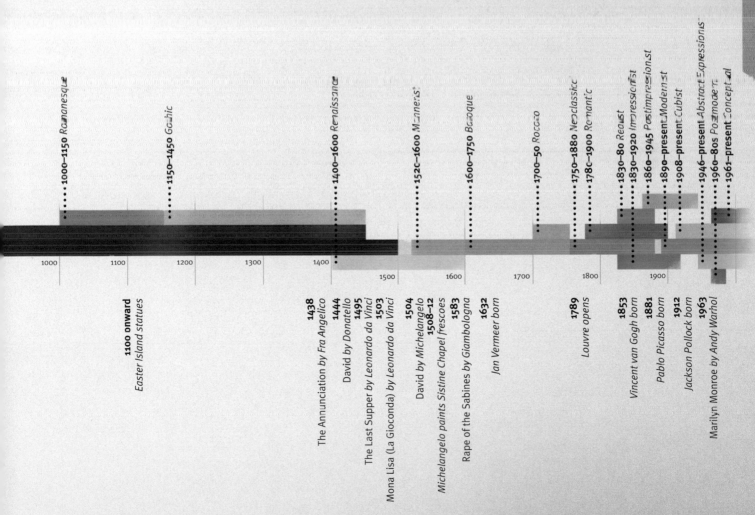

1000–1150 Romanesque

1150–1450 Gothic

1400–1600 Renaissance

1520–1600 Mannerist

1600–1750 Baroque

1700–50 Rococo

1750–1880 Neoclassic

178c–1900 Romantic

1830–80 Realist

1830–1920 Impressionist

1860–1945 Postimpressionist

1890–present Modernist

1908–present Cubist

1946–present Abstract Expressionism

1960–80s Postmodern

1961–present Conceptual

1100 onward
Easter Island statues

1438
The Annunciation by Fra Angelico

1444
David by Donatello

1495
The Last Supper by Leonardo da Vinci

1503
Mona Lisa (La Gioconda) by Leonardo da Vinci

1504
David by Michelangelo

1508–12
Michelangelo paints Sistine Chapel frescoes

1583
Rape of the Sabines by Giambologna

1632
Jan Vermeer born

1789
Louvre opens

1853
Vincent van Gogh born

1881
Pablo Picasso born

1912
Jackson Pollock born

1963
Marilyn Monroe by Andy Warhol

The Sound of Music_

From the banging of sticks on stretched animal skin right through to the banging of bones on rock, music—from a Greek term meaning "art for the muses"—has had a massive impact on human culture.

It is impossible to know how music first became such an important part of our lives, but it is clear that nature provides ample examples—from birdsong to the rhythmic chirping of insects.

A major movement of music is **classical** and, as a whole, it covers a period of over 1,500 years. While the development of styles over this period, up to the beginning of the twentieth century, was relatively slow and restrained, since 1900 there have been many varied developments.

Thanks to the number of radio and television stations now available, it is possible at any time of day or night to hear examples of all the musical genres seen on this page, going all the way back to the medieval period.

33,000 BC
A flute made of hollowed-out bones is one of the earliest musical instruments discovered. It is believed to be about 35,000 years old and was played by Neanderthals.

175 BC
Mawangui silk texts: Written on silk, these Chinese philosophical works were found in a tomb in the city of Changsha, Hunan, in 1973.

850
Historians uncover evidence of the earliest known mechanical instrument—a water-powered organ that played interchangeable cylinders automatically.

1764
Wolfgang Amadeus Mozart writes his first symphony at the age of eight.

1781
Mozart moves to Vienna and premieres his masterpiece The Marriage of Figaro.

1809–present
The brass band style is popularized.

1877
Thomas Edison invents the phonograph. He tests the machine using the nursery rhyme "Mary Had a Little Lamb."

1919
The theremin is invented by Russian professor Léon Theremin and is cited as one of the first electronic musical instruments, and the first ever that is played without being touched.

250 BC
Greek writings on music found.

AD 500–1760
Early classical period: This period can be divided into three subsets:
500–1400 Medieval
1400–1600 Renaissance
1600–1760 Baroque

1750–1820
The music that was dominant during this time can be characterized by simple melodies and sonatas. Most composers used the piano to write their pieces.

1773
The waltz becomes popular in Vienna.

1801
Beethoven performs his Symphony #1 in C Major for the first time in Vienna.

1860
The earliest recordings of a human voice are recorded on a phonautograph by Edouard-Léon Scott de Martinville, but the sounds cannot be played back.

1890
Blues music develops, predominately in the Deep South of the United States.

1924
The first high-fidelity sound recording is made using equipment that minimized

Something to Think About . . .

In 2008, 95 percent of all music that was downloaded from the Internet was illegally sourced, and it is estimated that on an average teenager's iPod, 800 of the songs are pirated. In 2010, iTunes—the world's most popular online digital media store—announced that it had sold 10 billion songs in under seven years.

A timeline of some of music's greatest achievements

magnetic tape is invented, revolutionizing the recording and broadcasting of music.

1935
The first reel-to-reel tape recorder—known as the K1—is demonstrated using magnetic tape invented by German-Austrian engineer Fritz Pfleumer.

1948
Record company Columbia introduces the first LP (long-playing) record. It can play 17 minutes of music on each side.

1963
At age 13, Stevie Wonder has his first major hit, "Fingertips (Pt. 2)," which was recorded when he was 12.

1966
Bob Goldstein coins the word "multimedia."

1977
Punk music changes the musical landscape.

1982
Michael Jackson releases Thriller. The album is still ranked as one of the best-selling albums of all time, due in part to the accompanying seven music videos of singles taken from the album.

1999
Shawn Fanning and Shaun Parker create Napster, the first file-sharing program for digital audio players.

2008
In November, for the first time, music downloads via the Internet outsell CDs. iTunes announces it has sold over a billion songs through the iTunes store.

1934
The Hammond electric organ is invented by American engineer Laurens Hammond.

1946
Elvis Presley is bought his first guitar from a Tupelo hardware store; it cost $12.95.

1951
Computer programmer Geoff Hill programs a computer in Australia to perform a melody—the first demonstration of computer-generated music.

1964
The Beatles perform to 73 million viewers on The Ed Sullivan Show.

1976–1982
Manufacturers Phillips and Sony develop the first type of compact disc.

1981
MTV is launched. The first video shown is "Video Killed the Radio Star" by the Buggles.

1994
The Rolling Stones become the first band to perform live over Internet radio.

2001
Apple launches the sleek iPod—a portable digital media player.

2010
Teenage pop star Justin Bieber's videos are viewed over a billion times on YouTube.

Great Reads in Time

The best-selling books of all time

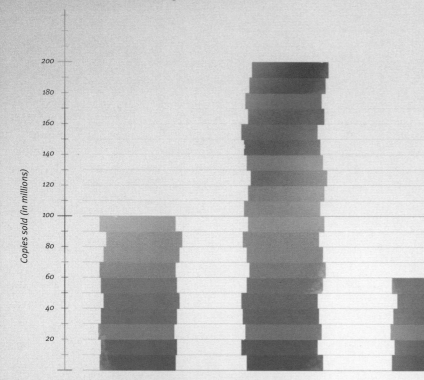

Copies sold (in millions)

The Dream of the Red Chamber (1791) Cao Xueqin
100 million copies sold
Xueqin wrote only the first 80
of its 120 chapters.

A Tale of Two Cities (1859) Charles Dickens
200 million copies sold
Issued as 31 weekly installments in
Dickens's magazine *All the Year Round*.

Heidi (1880) Johanna Spyri
60 million copies sold
Two sequels were written by the book's
English translator in the 1930s.
Neither sequel was endorsed by Spyri.

She (1887) H. Rider Haggard
65 million copies sold
"She" is short for "She who
must be obeyed."

Le Petit Prince (1943) Antoine de Saint-Exupéry
80 million copies sold
Le Petit Prince (The Little Prince) is set on Asteroid
B-612. A real asteroid discovered in 1993,
46610 Besixdouze, was named as a tribute.

Something to Think About . . .

While the Bible has sold over four billion copies to date, J. K. Rowling's series of seven Harry Potter books is the best-selling series in modern times, selling over 450 million books since *Harry Potter and the Philosopher's Stone* in 1997, as well as spawning a multibillion-dollar Hollywood film franchise.

The Lion, the Witch, and the Wardrobe (1950) C. S. Lewis
85 million copies sold
The first in the series of seven books covering the Chronicles of Narnia. Lewis died on the day that John F. Kennedy was assassinated.

The Catcher in the Rye (1951) J. D. Salinger
120 million copies sold
John Lennon's killer, Mark Chapman, was carrying a copy when he shot the rock star in 1980.

The Lord of the Rings (1955) J. R. R. Tolkien
150 million copies sold
The Lord of the Rings took 12 years to write and six more before it was published.

The Alchemist (1988) Paulo Coelho
65 million copies sold
The most translated novel by a living author. Coelho has a blog from where it is possible to download some of his novels for free.

The da Vinci Code (2003) Dan Brown
80 million copies sold
Although clearly a work of fiction, the book has created a campaign of denial among some Christian groups.

The Dawn of Television_

In the developed world, almost every house has one, and many have more than one. The television, invented in 1925 by Scotsman **John Logie Baird**, has taken over the world in less than a century and has changed the way we live.

The average viewer will watch over twenty hours of television per week. Other than working and sleeping, it is the activity we spend most of our time doing. When we are not watching television, we spend a lot of time talking about the programs we have seen.

While viewing figures and **television ownership** were already high, the introduction of **satellite television** and the expansion of the number of channels available has given sales of television sets a further boost. With so many options, it is not uncommon for the members of an average family to all be watching different programs at the same time. In the United States, for instance, over 75 percent of households have more than one set and over 50 percent have three or more.

1900 Russian scientist Constantin Perskyi coins the word "television."

1906 Russian scientist Boris Rosing builds the first mechanical television set incorporating a cathode-ray tube.

October 1925 Scottish inventor John Logie Baird gives the first demonstration of moving images on a television set.

1928 American Charles Jenkins opens the first television station.

March 1930 BBC begins test broadcasts in the UK.

1936 BBC begins broadcasts from Alexandra Palace. There are still fewer than 1,000 sets worldwide.

1936 First televised sports event — the Berlin Olympics.

1940 American Peter Goldmark (who works for the CBS network) invents color television.

1939–45 Television transmission halted almost everywhere during World War II.

1941 Bulova watches are advertised — the first television commercial. Twenty seconds cost $9.

1946 John Logie Baird dies.

October 1947 President Harry S. Truman broadcasts from the White House for the first time.

1949 1,000,000 television sets in the United States.

1951 10,000,000 television sets in the United States.

June 1952
The Guiding Light premieres on U.S. television. It becomes the world's longest-running soap opera, ending in September 2009.

1953
25,000,000 television sets in the United States.

1954
World Cup soccer televised.

1954
Color introduced to sets in the United States.

1960
Coronation Street begins in the UK. It is the longest-running soap still on air.

1962
Telstar—the first satellite to relay television—is launched.

July 1969
The Moon landing is watched by 600 million people.

September 1997
Two billion people watch Princess Diana's funeral.

2007
Bullfighting taken off state-run Spanish television.

2009
Televisions with 3-D capability go on sale.

Something to Think About . . .

In 1982 Seiko produced a television watch.
The screen was 1.5 inches.

The Introduction of Cinema_

Many people consider the 1906 Australian film *The Story of the Kelly Gang* to be the first feature-length film. Running at seventy minutes, it was much longer than anything that had come before, and it hit the screens just over ten years after the French **Lumière brothers invented cinema** as we know it.

Since Auguste and Louis Lumière held their first public screening in 1895, there have really only been **two major advances** in cinema. *Don Juan* was the first film to have **synchronized sound**, although it had no dialogue. The first "real" talkie was *The Jazz Singer*, released a year later in 1927. Many film stars' careers ended with the introduction of sound, but the industry as a whole never looked back.

The other major advance came with the **arrival of color**. A two-color system had been in use since the 1910s, but full three-color production did not arrive until 1932 with Disney's *Flowers and Trees*.

Since then, there have been further advances mainly to do with the size and shape of the projected image. A big obsession has always been with **three-dimensional** (3-D) screening. This technology has been around since the 1920s and had a first golden era in the 1950s, after which it went into decline until the early part of the twenty-first century, when it has entered again into the mainstream. Many blockbusters are now produced in both 2-D and 3-D formats.

Something to Think About . . .

The Academy Award of Merit is better known as an **Oscar**. The Academy of Motion Picture Arts and Sciences was formed in 1927.

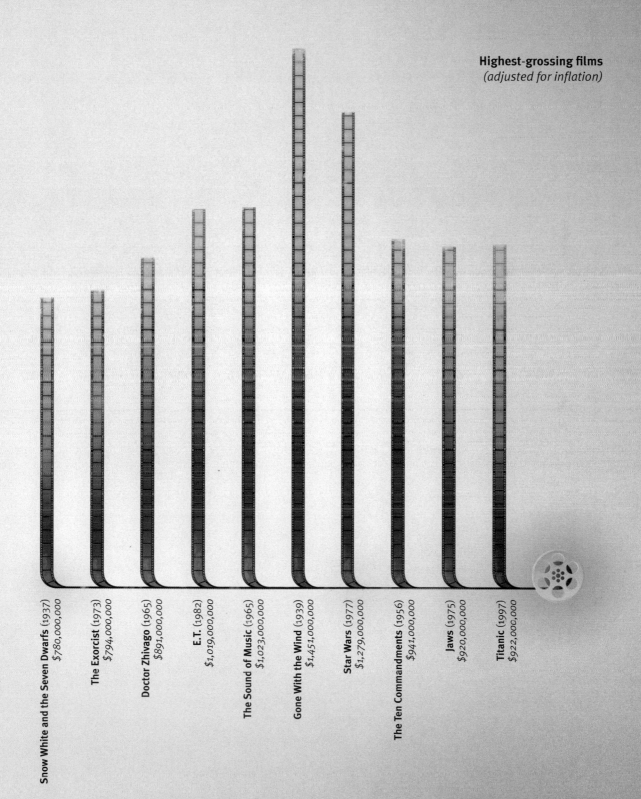

Highest-grossing films
(adjusted for inflation)

Snow White and the Seven Dwarfs (1937)
$780,000,000

The Exorcist (1973)
$794,000,000

Doctor Zhivago (1965)
$891,000,000

E.T. (1982)
$1,019,000,000

The Sound of Music (1965)
$1,023,000,000

Gone With the Wind (1939)
$1,451,000,000

Star Wars (1977)
$1,279,000,000

The Ten Commandments (1956)
$941,000,000

Jaws (1975)
$920,000,000

Titanic (1997)
$922,000,000

05.8 Sport's Date with History_

A timeline of some of sport's greatest moments

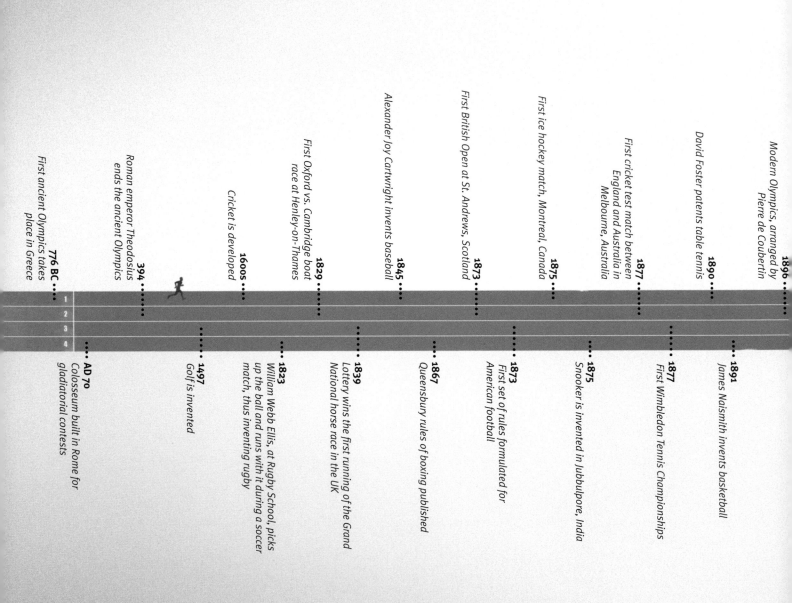

776 BC
First ancient Olympics takes place in Greece

394
Roman emperor Theodosius ends the ancient Olympics

1600s
Cricket is developed

1829
First Oxford vs. Cambridge boat race at Henley-on-Thames

1845
Alexander Joy Cartwright invents baseball

1873
First British Open at St. Andrews, Scotland

1875
First ice hockey match, Montreal, Canada

1877
First cricket test match between England and Australia in Melbourne, Australia

1890
David Foster patents table tennis

1896
Modern Olympics, arranged by Pierre de Coubertin

AD 70
Colosseum built in Rome for gladiatorial contests

1497
Golf is invented

1823
William Webb Ellis, at Rugby School, picks up the ball and runs with it during a soccer match, thus inventing rugby

1839
Lottery wins the first running of the Grand National horse race in the UK

1867
Queensbury rules of boxing published

1873
First set of rules formulated for American football

1875
Snooker is invented in Jubbulpore, India

1877
First Wimbledon Tennis Championships

1891
James Naismith invents basketball

132

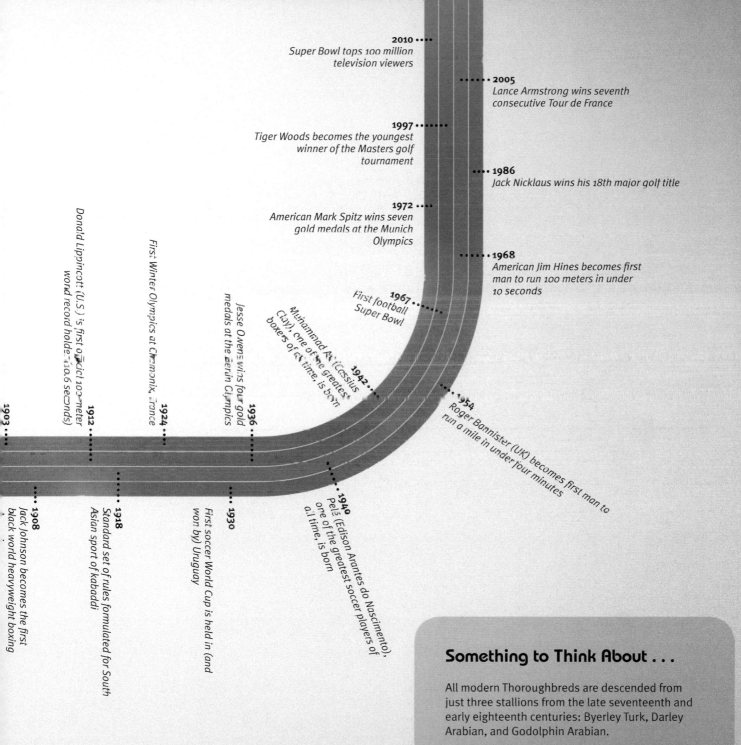

2010 • • • •
Super Bowl tops 100 million
television viewers

• • • • • • 2005
Lance Armstrong wins seventh
consecutive Tour de France

1997 • • • • • • •
Tiger Woods becomes the youngest
winner of the Masters golf
tournament

• • • 1986
Jack Nicklaus wins his 18th major golf title

1972 • • • •
American Mark Spitz wins seven
gold medals at the Munich
Olympics

• • • • 1968
American Jim Hines becomes first
man to run 100 meters in under
10 seconds

1967 • • •
First football
Super Bowl

1942
Muhammad Ali (Cassius
Clay), one of the greatest
boxers of all time, is born

1954
Roger Bannister (UK) becomes first man to
run a mile in under four minutes

1940
Pelé (Edison Arantes do Nascimento),
one of the greatest soccer players of
all time, is born

1936
Jesse Owens wins four gold
medals at the Berlin Olympics

1930
First soccer World Cup is held in (and
won by) Uruguay

1924
First Winter Olympics at Chamonix, France

1918
Standard set of rules formulated for South
Asian sport of kabaddi

1912
Donald Lippincott (U.S.) is first official 100-meter
world record holder (10.6 seconds)

1908
Jack Johnson becomes the first
black world heavyweight boxing

1903

Something to Think About . . .

All modern Thoroughbreds are descended from
just three stallions from the late seventeenth and
early eighteenth centuries: Byerley Turk, Darley
Arabian, and Godolphin Arabian.

05.9 Languages of the World_

Humans started talking 150,000 years ago . . . and we haven't shut up since.

It is often said that the United States and England are two countries separated by a common language; across the entire planet, however, there are nearly 7,000 languages being spoken today.

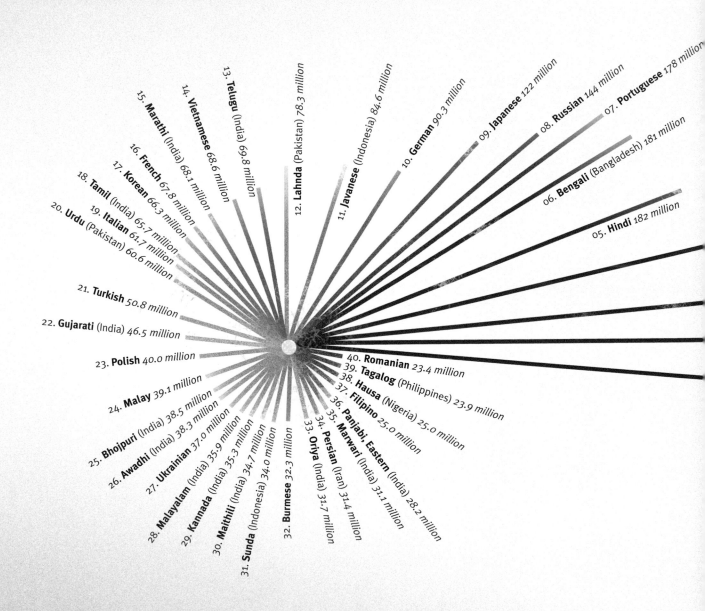

05. **Hindi** 182 million
06. **Bengali** (Bangladesh) 181 million
07. **Portuguese** 178 million
08. **Russian** 144 million
09. **Japanese** 122 million
10. **German** 90.3 million
11. **Javanese** (Indonesia) 84.6 million
12. **Lahnda** (Pakistan) 78.3 million
13. **Telugu** (India) 69.8 million
14. **Vietnamese** 68.6 million
15. **Marathi** (India) 68.1 million
16. **French** 67.8 million
17. **Korean** 66.3 million
18. **Tamil** (India) 65.7 million
19. **Italian** 61.7 million
20. **Urdu** (Pakistan) 60.6 million
21. **Turkish** 50.8 million
22. **Gujarati** (India) 46.5 million
23. **Polish** 40.0 million
24. **Malay** 39.1 million
25. **Bhojpuri** (India) 38.5 million
26. **Awadhi** (India) 38.3 million
27. **Ukrainian** 37.0 million
28. **Malayalam** (India) 35.9 million
29. **Kannada** (India) 35.3 million
30. **Maithili** (India) 34.7 million
31. **Sunda** (Indonesia) 34.0 million
32. **Burmese** 32.3 million
33. **Oriya** (India) 31.7 million
34. **Persian** (Iran) 31.4 million
35. **Marwari** (India) 31.1 million
36. **Panjabi, Eastern** (India) 28.2 million
37. **Filipino** 25.0 million
38. **Hausa** (Nigeria) 25.0 million
39. **Tagalog** (Philippines) 23.9 million
40. **Romanian** 23.4 million

Something to Think About . . .

Of the almost 7,000 languages in the world, more than half are expected to die out within the next 100 years. This trend was illustrated by the death of Marie Smith Jones in Anchorage, Alaska, in 2008 at the age of eighty-nine. She is believed to have been the last native speaker of the Eyak language, once spoken in southern Alaska near the mouth of the Copper River. In her later years, she helped researchers at the University of Alaska compile an Eyak dictionary, so that it would have a chance of being revived in the future.

. **Arabic** 221 million

03. **English** 328 million

02. **Spanish** 329 million

01. **Chinese** (including Mandarin, Gan, Hakka, Huizhou, Jinyu, Min Bei, Min Dong, Min Nan, Min Zhong, Xiang, Wu, Yue) 1.2 billion

In many cases, the number of people who speak a country's language is almost equal to its population. This is because not many people outside of that country have it as a first language. Of all the languages, English and Spanish are the two that have most outstripped their native populations.

Pollution and the Planet_

In a recent list of the **world's top ten most polluted cities**, seven of them had gained their notoriety due to an increased dependency on **driving cars**. Part of the problem is that many people cannot afford to live in the city where they work, so they have to drive in to get to their jobs. This is *the* major concern in cities such as **Beijing, Cairo, Dhaka,** and **New Delhi**—and most especially in **Buenos Aires,** where the **population increases** fourfold during the daytime.

Tanzania's capital of **Dar Es Salaam** contains 80 percent of the country's industry, and the residents burn **waste and biomass** on the streets. **Moscow's** recent **forest fires** have added to its pollution, while **Mexico City** has a combination of industry and cars compounded by dry, hot spells that add to this pollution.

The last two cities in the hall of shame are **Dzerzhinsk** in Russia and China's **Linfen**. Dzerzhinsk is where the Soviet Union produced many of its biological and chemical weapons during the Cold War up until the 1990s. This "secret" city is still suffering from the poor management of this **industrial output**. Linfen, officially the most polluted city in the world, has the simple combination of cars, high population, and **coal-fired power stations** to blame.

The world's top six most harmful pollutants

	Caused by	Major problem
1. Carbon dioxide	*Burning fossil fuels and deforestation*	*Increases global warming*
2. Nitrogen dioxide	*Burning fossil fuels*	*Attacks Earth's protective ozone layer*
3. Particulate matter	*Roads, fires, construction*	*Gets into the lungs*
4. Sulfur dioxide and chlorofluorocarbons	*Burning fossil fuels*	*Constricts tubes in the lungs*
5. Lead	*Industry (used to be in gasoline)*	*Affects the nervous system, kidney function, and immune system, among others*
6. Carbon monoxide	*Mainly from automobile exhausts*	*Reduces oxygen intake*

Rest of the world *32.93%*

Something to Think About . . .

In December 1952, there was a buildup of smog in London.
It is estimated that 4,000 people died as a direct result of
this polluted air. It led to the 1956 Clean Air Act.

The world's top ten worst polluters
In global percentage and annual CO_2 emissions
(in thousands of tons)

6. **Germany** 2.69%
(787,936)

7. **Canada** 1.90%
(557,340)

8. **United Kingdom** 1.84%
(539,617)

5. **Japan** 4.08%
(1,234,545)

9. **South Korea** 1.72%
(503,321)

4. **Russia** 5.24%
(1,537,357)

10. **Iran** 1.69%
(495,987)

3. **India** 5.50%
(1,612,362)

1. **China** 22.30%
(29,321,302)

2. **United States** 19.91%
(6,538,367)

05.11 Our Changing World: Global Warming_

The term "global warming" was first coined in 1975 by Wallace Broecker in an article he wrote for *Science* titled: "Climatic Change: Are We on the Brink of a Pronounced Global Warming?" **Climate change** and the effect it may have on the planet is one of the most pressing problems facing governments around the world, but this has not led to any decisive action.

The problem is that while the evidence shows that the **average global temperature has risen** by 1.4 degrees Fahrenheit since accurate records began in 1880, there is no real consensus on what the future consequences of further warming—or even what the future change—might be. This lack of agreement has meant that no clear strategy or desire for action to contain it has been reached by the world's most powerful industrial nations.

Scientists with a pessimistic view of our future predict that the speed of the rise in temperature is increasing, and may soon reach a point where the damage to the world's atmospheres, oceans, and **ecosystems is unrepairable**. The optimists, however, regard the planet as a **self-regulating entity** and believe that this current increase in temperature is no more than a blip that will turn the other way before long. Earth's meteorological history is full of these blips, say the optimists.

If the pessimists are to be believed and the increase continues, the effect on the planet could be catastrophic. For instance, with rainfall increasing, more flooding would occur, which would lead to an erosion of viable farming areas and thus, ultimately, a world food shortage. The level of the sea is also increased by the warming and the water from the **melting ice caps**.

Something to Think About . . .

One of the major stated causes of global warming is CO_2 emission. Cars, trains, and airplanes would top most people's list of the worst offenders, but not according to a 2008 UN report that found livestock to be the cause of 18 percent of global emissions. The methane from their digestive gases and manure contributes in a large way to this figure, as it is twenty times more damaging than carbon dioxide.

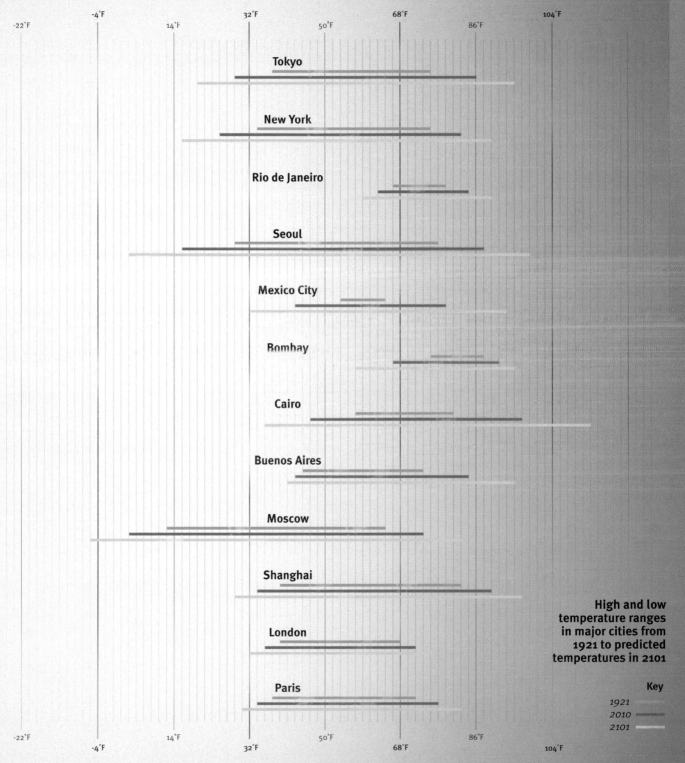

**High and low
temperature ranges
in major cities from
1921 to predicted
temperatures in 2101**

Key

1921
2010
2101

Seven Man-Made Wonders of the World_

Everything that you see around you is made from material that has always been here. When you think about that fact, it makes **human achievements** even more astonishing. *Apollo 11*, the first craft to leave our atmosphere and successfully land on the Moon, was built using raw materials that were, in effect, available to cavemen.

The Moon landing is no less incredible than the **Egyptian pyramids**. That they have lasted nearly 5,000 years and are the only remaining item from the mythical ancient wonders of the world is testament to their creators. And between these two events, humans have continually surpassed previous generations, leaving a legacy at which we can only marvel.

The seven man-made wonders of the world shown here are in no particular order.

Great Pyramids
c. 2560 BC
Giza, Egypt

Series of pyramids built for the Fourth Dynasty pharaoh Khufu. Notable for the astronomical connection to Orion's Belt.

Taj Mahal
1632–53
Agra, India

A mausoleum built by Shah Jaham in memory of his wife Mumtaz Mahal. Considered by many as one of the most beautiful man-made structures in the world, and a globally recognized symbol of eternal love.

Machu Picchu
15th century
Urubamba Valley, Peru

The Lost City of the Incas, as it is commonly referred to, had gone undiscovered by the rest of the world until 1911 and, even today, remains relatively intact.

Apollo 11
Landed on the Moon on July 20, 1969

The first craft—made by materials found on Earth—that traveled to another celestial body; the Moon is about 238,857 miles away. It returned home safely and marked a significant moment in human technological history.

Mount Rushmore
1941
Keystone, South Dakota

The heads of four important U.S. presidents—George Washington, Thomas Jefferson, Theodore Roosevelt, and Abraham Lincoln—carved into the granite rock of the Black Hills region of South Dakota. Each head is about sixty feet high; the monument was created as an attempt to improve tourism in the area. It worked.

Great Wall of China
5th century BC–16th century AD
China

This ancient wall meanders around northern China at about 5,500 miles in length and was built to defend the borders against nomadic invaders.

Stonehenge
c. 2700 BC
Wiltshire, United Kingdom

No one is exactly sure who made Stonehenge—or how.

Chapter 06.0 **Making History_**

The Spread of Humans Across the Globe_

A combination of **genetic study** (of mitochondrial DNA) and the discovery of **early human fossils** has allowed modern scientists to track humans' first migration patterns out of Africa—the continent many believe to be the birthplace of human life. Out of Africa, the spread of early humans across the globe was one of our most important evolutionary journeys and the first step to creating civilization.

52,000–45,000 ya
A mini ice age occurs, causing further movement of Homo sapiens *into Europe—up the Danube to Hungary and Austria.*

65,000–52,000 ya
The planet warms and groupings of Homo sapiens *start heading north to the Levant and into Europe.*

115,000–90,000 ya
The Levant group dies out due to a global freeze.

10,000–8,000 ya
Final collapse of the last ice age. Sahara desert region is characterized as a sloping grassland.

135,000–115,000 ya
Some groupings make far as the Levant—the jo point between western the eastern Mediterranea northeast Africa—throug open Northern Gate

160,000–135,000 ya
Four large groupings of Homo sapiens *travel to the Cape of Good Hope, Congo basin, Ivory Coast, and Herto, Ethiopia.*

160,000 ya
Homo sapiens *orig in East Africa and a into groupings*

Something to Think About . . .

While modern *Homo sapiens* has a desire to travel the globe for pleasure, the early spread of humanity across the planet was motivated primarily by the search for food and warmer climates. Nomadic tribes followed the migration patterns of the herd animals they hunted. The ability of early *Homo sapiens* to adapt and thrive in new and harsh conditions gave humans a key advantage over *Homo erectus* and set the course for global domination.

40,000–25,000 ya
*Central Asian groups move
toward Europe, north into the
Arctic Circle, and join eastern
Asians in the spread into
northeast Eurasia.*

45,000–40,000 ya
*Groups of Homo sapiens
from eastern Asian coast
move west to central Asia,
from Pakistan to central
Asia, and from Indochina to
the Qing-Hai Plateau.*

25,000–22,000 ya
*What will become Native
Americans cross the Bering
Land Bridge connecting
Siberia and Alaska.*

22,000–19,000 ya
*The last ice age occurs. North
American groups depopulate.
Some groups survive.*

12,500–10,000 ya
*North America is
repopulated.*

19,000–15,000 ya
*The last glacial maximum—a
period when huge areas of land
are covered in ice sheets—occurs.
In North America, south of the ice,
groups of Homo sapiens continue
to develop and diversify.*

85,000–75,000 ya
*From Sri Lanka, they
continue around the coast
all the way to southern
China.*

90,000–85,000 ya
*A grouping of Homo sapiens
crosses the mouth of the Red
Sea and heads along the coast to
India—all non-African humans are
descended from this group.*

15,000–12,500 ya
*Coastal routes open
around South America.*

74,000 ya
*Mount Toba (in Sumatra, western
Indonesia) erupts, creating a
nuclear winter and a 1,000-year-
long ice age. World population
drops below 10,000, and possibly
as low as 1,000 couples.*

74,000–65,000 ya
*The surviving groups spread
into Australia and New Guinea,
away from the intense cold of
the Lower Pleniglacial.*

(ya = years ago)   *Homo sapiens*   *Neanderthals*   Early hominids

06.2 The End of Nomadic Humans_

From the very earliest days of our evolution, humans were **hunter-gatherers** roaming from coast to coast, following the source of food and making camp wherever safe until all the nearby food ran out or had moved on. Then, about **10,000 years ago,** the nomadic lifestyle came to an end and early settlements were formed.

The catalyst for this **Neolithic revolution** was the end of the last ice age. As temperatures rose again, the supply of **animals and vegetation increased** and the need to move around as often decreased. Some groups found that they could remain in the same place for longer periods, and once they had survived a year in the same location, all the problems relating to that site through each of the seasons had been shown to be surmountable.

This period coincided with the realization that some animals were prepared to stay near human settlements when provided with feed. As long as they were provided nourishment, the animals would not move on and **subsistence farming** was created. It didn't necessarily work everywhere it was tried, but when it didn't, the people just moved on and tried it somewhere else.

Factors that were likely to increase the likelihood of early settlements were the **availability of fresh water** and the **abundance of edible flora**.

Something to Think About . . .

One of the first results of the lifestyle change from hunter-gatherer to early settler was a rise in disease due to an increased lack of variation in the diet. However, settling did result in a growth in population because it was suddenly easier to look after infants when people were not constantly on the move.

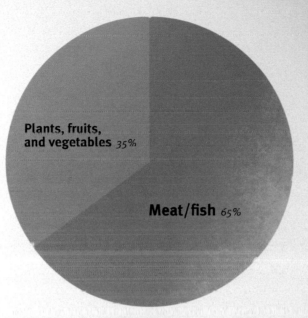

Changes in diet from early humans to the present day

Plants, fruits, and vegetables *35%*

Meat/fish *65%*

Hunter-gatherer
High in protein, low in carbohydrates

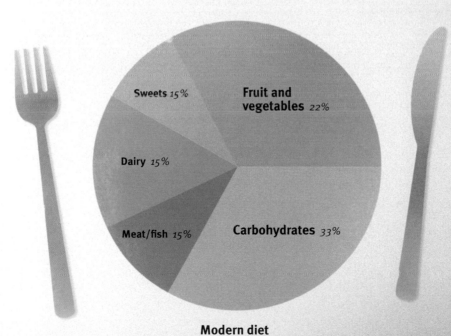

Sweets *15%*

Fruit and vegetables *22%*

Dairy *15%*

Carbohydrates *33%*

Meat/fish *15%*

Modern diet
Low in protein, high in carbohydrates

The Empires_

They came, they saw, they conquered.

Throughout history, powerful countries have made the decision to spread their control beyond their own borders. This empire building, by its nature, generally requires the use of force—be it **military or political**. King Sargon the Great built the first empire around the city of Akkad (Iraq) in 2300 BC. The last empire in the truest sense of the term was the Soviet Union, which finally broke up in the early 1990s. The importance of these empires is that they **exported their culture**, beliefs, and language to the territories they conquered. In some cases these influences held—the Spanish culture in Argentina is a perfect example.

Roman Empire · · · · ·
27 BC–AD 474

Capital:
Rome
Coverage at maximum extent:
North to Scotland, south to Sudan, west to Portugal and Morocco, east to Iraq and Azerbaijan
Main contribution to their colonies:
Modern language

200 BC   100 BC   AD 100

Egyptian Empire · · · · ·
16th–11th centuries BC

Capital:
Thebes for the most part, but also Akhetaten and Pi-Ramesses at different times
Coverage at maximum extent:
North and east to Syria, south to Sudan, west to Libya
Main contribution to their colonies:
The Pyramids

Ancient Greece · · · · ·
5th–4th centuries BC

Capital:
Athens
Coverage at maximum extent:
North to Ukraine, south to Libya, west to Spain, east to the east coast of the Black Sea
Main contribution to their colonies:
Philosophy

Chinese Empire
221 BC–AD 1911

Capital:
Mainly Beijing
Coverage at maximum extent:
Mainly within the borders of what we now call China
Main contribution to their colonies:
Bureaucracy

Spanish Empire
1521–1643

Capital:
Madrid
Coverage at maximum extent:
*To the west encompassing North and South America
(apart from Brazil), the Philippines to the east,
small pockets of Africa and India*
Main contribution to their colonies:
Roman Catholicism

Mongol Empire
1206–1368

Capital:
Zhongdu (modern-day Beijing)
Coverage at maximum extent:
*North to Russia, south to Korea and Pakistan,
west to Poland, east to China*
Main contribution to their colonies:
Organized warfare

British Empire
Late 16th century–mid-20th century

Capital:
London
Coverage at maximum extent:
*West to Canada and eastern America, south to South Africa,
east to New Zealand and Australia, India*
Main contribution to their colonies:
Constitutional government

History of Modern Warfare_

The first recorded war in history was between Sumer (now in Iraq) and Elam (Iran), and occurred around 2700 BC. Since this date, there has not been a day when there has not been a war taking place somewhere on Earth.

The spoils of war may well usually be **material possessions**, but war is also heavily dictated by philosophical disputes over the aggressor's disapproval of the **way of life** of the opposition and a strong desire to impose its own set of values.

While there has always been war, it was due to improved communication and transportation that the world was able to have a **full-scale conflict** that involved almost every continent. World War I began in the summer of 1914 and concluded in late 1918. Just twenty-one years later, another global conflict began in 1939 and lasted until 1945. World War II was only finally ended by the United States' use of the atomic bomb, and at the time there was a feeling that with this threat hanging over the planet, the days of global conflicts were over. Sadly, this proved to be a false hope.

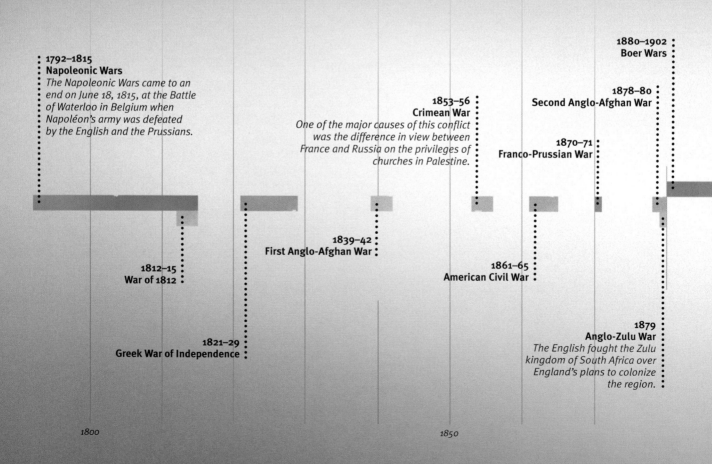

1792–1815
Napoleonic Wars
The Napoleonic Wars came to an end on June 18, 1815, at the Battle of Waterloo in Belgium when Napoléon's army was defeated by the English and the Prussians.

1812–15
War of 1812

1821–29
Greek War of Independence

1839–42
First Anglo-Afghan War

1853–56
Crimean War
One of the major causes of this conflict was the difference in view between France and Russia on the privileges of churches in Palestine.

1861–65
American Civil War

1870–71
Franco-Prussian War

1878–80
Second Anglo-Afghan War

1879
Anglo-Zulu War
The English fought the Zulu kingdom of South Africa over England's plans to colonize the region.

1880–1902
Boer Wars

1800

1850

Something to Think About . . .

Mutually assured destruction, generally abbreviated as MAD, is the theory by which peace is maintained due to the knowledge that if either side attacks the other, both sides will be annihilated.

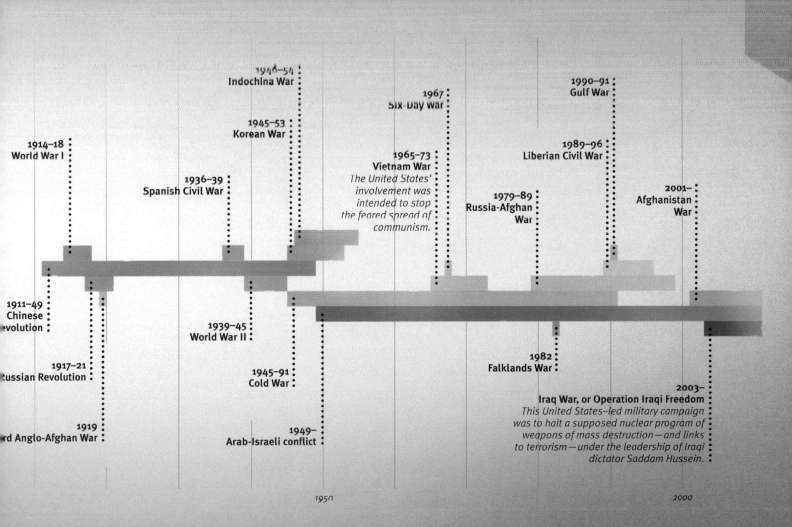

1914–18
World War I

1911–49
Chinese
Revolution

1917–21
Russian Revolution

1919
Third Anglo-Afghan War

1936–39
Spanish Civil War

1939–45
World War II

1945–53
Korean War

1946–54
Indochina War

1945–91
Cold War

1949–
Arab-Israeli conflict

1967
Six-Day War

1965–73
Vietnam War
*The United States'
involvement was
intended to stop
the feared spread of
communism.*

1979–89
Russia-Afghan
War

1982
Falklands War

1990–91
Gulf War

1989–96
Liberian Civil War

2001–
Afghanistan
War

2003–
Iraq War, or Operation Iraqi Freedom
*This United States–led military campaign
was to halt a supposed nuclear program of
weapons of mass destruction—and links
to terrorism—under the leadership of Iraqi
dictator Saddam Hussein.*

The Five Years of World War I_

On the June 28, 1914, Gavrilo Princip, a Bosnian-Serb, shot dead **Archduke Franz Ferdinand**, the heir to the Hapsburg Empire. This event is usually cited as the primary cause of the war; however, in effect, it was the straw that broke the back of a **delicate balance of alliances and treaties**. It led, like the toppling of one domino onto another, to the **collapse of world peace** and a conflict that lasted for five years.

At the center of the conflict was Germany, concerned by the powers on either side, **France and Russia**, and jealous of **Britain's dominance of the seas**. France harbored a long-term hostility toward Germany dating back to the **Franco-Prussian War**. Meanwhile, Russia and the Austro-Hungarian Empire were both trying to **gain supremacy** in the Balkans.

The archduke's death led to a declaration of war on Serbia by Austria. Germany, having promised support for Austria-Hungary, declared war on Russia, then on France. The German invasion of Belgium triggered the terms of the **1839 Treaty of London**, meaning Britain was obliged to declare war on Germany. Only five weeks after Princip pulled the trigger, the **world was at war**. Five years to the day after that shot was fired, the war was finally concluded with the signing of the **Treaty of Versailles**.

June 28, 1914
Assassination of Archduke Franz Ferdinand, heir to the empire of Hapsburg.

July 28, 1914
Austria declares war on Serbia.

August 1, 1914
Germany declares war on Russia.

August 3, 1914
Germany declares war on France, then invades Belgium.

August 4, 1914
Britain declares war on Germany.

October 29, 1914
Turkey joins forces with the Germans, forming the Central Powers—one of the two sides that fought in the war. The opposing side was the Allied Powers formed of England, France, and the Russian Empire.

May 23, 1915
Italy declares war on Germany and Austria.

Something to Think About . . .

Nearly 10 million soldiers died and 21 million were wounded during World War I. A total of 65 million soldiers were mobilized for the conflict.

April 6, 1917
The United States declares war on Germany.

December 5, 1917
Armistice between Germany and Russia.

March 3, 1918
Germany and Russia sign Treaty of Brest-Litovsk, marking Russia's exit from the war.

October 30, 1918
Turkey makes peace with the Allied Powers.

November 3, 1918
Austria makes peace with the Allied Powers.

November 11, 1918
Germany signs the armistice. The end of World War I is announced.

June 28, 1919
The Treaty of Versailles is signed by Germany and the Allied Powers.

06.6 World War II _

World War I was often referred to as "the war to end all wars." This proved to be far from true, and just twenty years after the signing of the **Treaty of Versailles**, Germany's invasion of Poland forced Britain into declaring war.

Many things led indirectly to this breaking point, but much of the blame for the eventual conflict has been placed at the door of Versailles. By imposing economical and social conditions upon Germany, which at the time seemed fair (but have since been reevaluated as harsh), the seeds were sown for a second war. The resentment Germany's people and politicians felt toward these punishments, combined with the difficulty the country had in repairing its **economy after World War I**, created a fertile ground for the rise of the National Socialists and **Hitler's Nazi party**.

World War II began on **September 3, 1939**, when Britain and France declared war on Germany two days after the German army invaded Poland. It was not until Japan attacked the United States in December 1941 that the United States joined the Allied forces.

Germany surrendered on May 7, 1945. Japan followed on August 14 after Hiroshima and Nagasaki had been **annihilated by atomic bombs** dropped by the U.S. Army.

In all, **50 million people died** during the conflict. Only 30 percent of these casualties were soldiers. Russia suffered the biggest losses (20 million dead), while the Nazi Holocaust saw the murder of 6 million Jews.

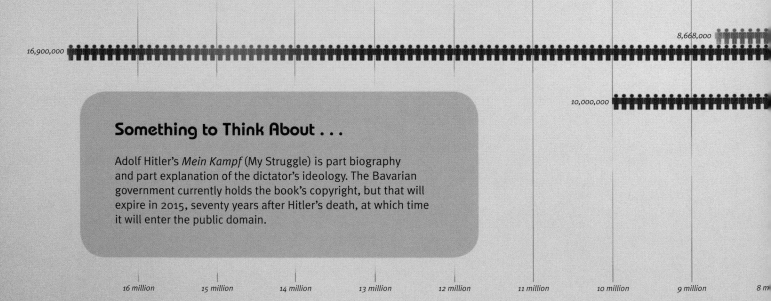

16,900,000

8,668,000

10,000,000

Something to Think About . . .

Adolf Hitler's *Mein Kampf* (My Struggle) is part biography and part explanation of the dictator's ideology. The Bavarian government currently holds the book's copyright, but that will expire in 2015, seventy years after Hitler's death, at which time it will enter the public domain.

16 million   15 million   14 million   13 million   12 million   11 million   10 million   9 million   8 m

Military and civilian deaths during World War II

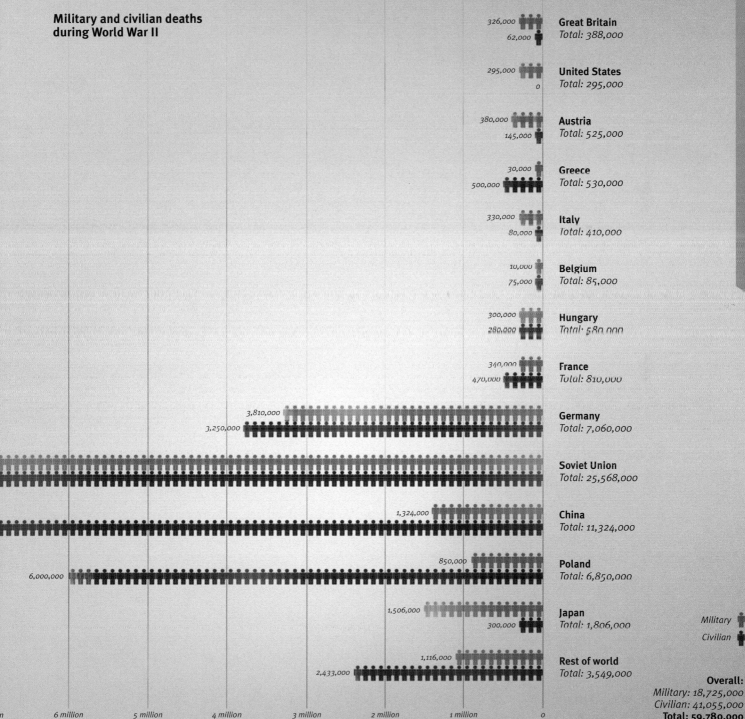

	Deaths	
Great Britain	326,000 (military)	62,000 (civilian) — Total: 388,000
United States	295,000	0 — Total: 295,000
Austria	380,000	145,000 — Total: 525,000
Greece	30,000	500,000 — Total: 530,000
Italy	330,000	80,000 — Total: 410,000
Belgium	10,000	75,000 — Total: 85,000
Hungary	300,000	280,000 — Total: 580,000
France	340,000	470,000 — Total: 810,000
Germany	3,810,000	3,250,000 — Total: 7,060,000
Soviet Union		Total: 25,568,000
China	1,324,000	Total: 11,324,000
Poland	850,000	6,000,000 — Total: 6,850,000
Japan	1,506,000	300,000 — Total: 1,806,000
Rest of world	1,116,000	2,433,000 — Total: 3,549,000

Military
Civilian

Scale: 6 million · 5 million · 4 million · 3 million · 2 million · 1 million · 0

Overall:
Military: 18,725,000
Civilian: 41,055,000
Total: 59,780,000

Powerful Leaders of the Past 2,000 Years_

Winston Churchill said that "history is written by the victors," but this doesn't stop some of the defeated from entering the ranks of the **history makers**. If evil things happen because good people do nothing, then it is fair to say that some of our most famous figures would not have come to the fore without the catalyst of the evil they fought.

Churchill himself is a good example of this. While he was prominent in British politics before World War II, he would not be the iconic figure he became without the "help" of German dictator Adolf Hitler.

Throughout history, there have been "good" leaders and "evil" leaders. Whichever side of the **moral compass** they stood upon, they all had one thing in common: the ability to make others follow them. This capacity may have stemmed from charisma or intellect, or it may have been fear that made their followers fall into line.

Queen Victoria

Born/died: *1819–1901*
In power: *1837–1901*
Role: *Queen of Great Britain and the ruler of the British Empire*
Followers: *400 million*
Known for: *Overseeing Britain's age of industrial revolution, global economic progress, and expansion of the empire.*

Mohandas Gandhi

Born/died: *1869–1948*
In power: *1915–1948*
Role: *Father of India*
Followers: *310 million*
Known for: *Helping India gain independence from the British and inspiring his millions of followers in the power of nonviolent civil disobedience.*

Jesus Christ

Born/died: *c. 6 BC–AD 35*
In power: *AD 30–present*
Role: *Catalyst for foundation of Christianity*
Followers: *2 billion*
Known for: *Being the son of God, sacrificing himself for humanity, the resurrection, and creating Christianity.*

Genghis Khan

Born/died: *1162–1227*
In power: *1206–1227*
Role: *Founder of Mongol Empire*
Followers: *100 million*
Known for: *Born in Mongolia, Genghis Khan is often cited for his great military prowess and expanding his empire over almost all of Asia by the time of his death.*

Adolf Hitler

Born/died: *1889–1945*
In power: *1933–1945*
Role: *Chancellor and Führer*
Followers: *90 million*
Known for: *Ruled Germany for twelve years as a leader for poor Germans after World War I, led the Nazi party, and authorized the annihilation of 6 million Jews via the Holocaust.*

Julius Caesar

Born/died: *100–44 BC*
In power: *48–44 BC*
Role: *Ruler of Roman Empire*
Followers: *55 million*
Known for: *A highly respected Roman general and military strategist, credited with developing the expansion of Roman civilization around Europe.*

Attila the Hun

Born/died: *406–453*
In power: *433–453*
Role: *Ruler of the Hun Empire*
Followers: *Unknown*
Known for: *Often referred to as the "Scourge of God," Atilla was a powerful military strategist who killed his own brother so that he did not have to share ruling the empire.*

Martin Luther King Jr.

Born/died: *1929–1968*
In power: *1957–1968*
Role: *Prominent leader in the African American civil rights movement*
Followers: *Unknown*
Known for: *His "I Have a Dream" speech in 1963 led to him becoming the youngest recipient of the Nobel Peace Prize in 1964. He was assassinated in 1968.*

Winston Churchill

Born/died: *1874–1965*
In power: *1940–45, 1951–55*
Role: *Prime minister of Great Britain*
Followers: *46 million*
Known for: *Leading the British, along with help from the rest of the allies, to victory against the Germans in World War II.*

The Rise of the Superpowers_

A superpower is described as a nation that has the ability to **influence global events** and the **behavior of less-significant nations**. For a long period after World War II, there were only two nations that fell into this category: the Soviet Union (USSR) and the United States. For nearly forty years, they held the balance of world power between them, and the Cold War in which they were involved threatened the future of the planet.

With the collapse of communism between 1989 and 1991, and the subsequent destruction of the USSR, the **power balance** of the world **shifted and fragmented** to such an extent that **the number of superpowers has risen**. What makes a superpower can subtly shift on an almost daily basis, but it is generally accepted that there are currently five.

The United States has held its place at the top table, and Russia has taken the still slightly warm seat once held by the USSR. Joining these two are China, with 20 percent of the world's population, India with over 17 percent, and the European Union (EU) with over a quarter of the world's gross domestic product (GDP).

With a burgeoning economy, Brazil is pushing for a place as a superpower, as is Japan, and within the next decade or so the number of superpowers in the world could increase to ten. At that point, a new term will perhaps need to be coined.

The United States' total military expenditure in 2009 was around seven times more than that of China.

United States
Population: *307,000,000*
GDP: *$14,000,000,000,000*
Nuclear weapons capability: *Yes*
Military expenditures (2009): *$663,255,000,000*
Tourist visits per year: *54,900,000*

Something to Think About . . .

The EU is counted as a single entity because of the agreement between the member nations that holds it together. This includes a single currency, the euro (although not every member uses it), and a European parliament, which has power over all the members.

European Union
Population: *500,000,000*
GDP: *$16,000,000,000,000*
Nuclear weapons capability: *Yes*
Military expenditures (2009):
France $67,316,000,000, UK $69,271,000,000
Tourist visits per year: *France 74,200,000*

Russia
Population: *142,000,000*
GDP: *$1,300,000,000,000*
Nuclear weapons capability: *Yes*
Military expenditures (2009): *$61,000,000,000*
Tourist visits per year: *20,600,000*

*France is the most popular tourist
destination in the world.*

China
Population: *1,325,000,000*
GDP: *$5,000,000,000,000*
Nuclear weapons capability: *Yes*
Military expenditures (2009): *$98,800,000,000*
Tourist visits per year: *50,900,000*

India
Population: *1,140,000,000*
GDP: *$1,250,000,000,000*
Nuclear weapons capability: *Yes*
Military expenditures (2009): *$36,600,000,000*
Tourist visits per year: *5,000,000*

06.9 The Fall of Communism_

Like two playing cards balanced against one another, the United States and the Soviet Union dictated the security of the world for forty years after the end of World War II. Like playing cards themselves, this was a delicate balance and the house of cards could have toppled at any moment. When the Soviet Union and the communist bloc disintegrated at the end of the 1980s, the world changed forever.

The house of cards analogy has probably never been more apt than when used to describe the **collapse of communism**. During the 1980s, the communist government in Poland faced major anticommunist opposition, and when the **trade unions won in the elections**, the first card fell. Developments in global communication meant it was possible to broadcast this news in spite of state ownership of domestic media channels, and it was only two months before Hungary went the same way.

Hungary's political shift opened up a route for dissatisfied East Germans to enter West Germany and thus precipitated **the fall of the Berlin Wall**. As the wall was a major symbol of the **East–West political divide**, its demolition was vital in increasing the momentum for anticommunist ideals, and by July 1991 the Warsaw Pact, the communist bloc's equivalent to NATO, was dissolved and the Soviet Union was no more.

Something to Think About . . .

After World War II, Germany was divided into East and West Germany. East Germany followed the sociopolitical ideologies of the communist Soviet Union, while West Germany followed the democratic principles of the West. The Berlin Wall, which divided the two countries, was a physical symbol of what Winston Churchill called the "Iron Curtain" that separated Europe after 1945.

Former Soviet Union countries *(by population percentage)*

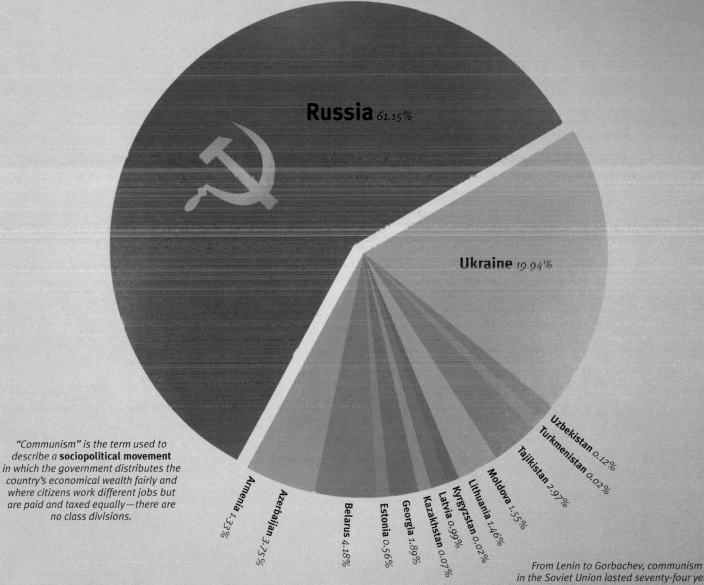

Russia *61.15%*

Ukraine *19.94%*

Uzbekistan *0.12%*

Turkmenistan *0.02%*

Tajikistan *2.97%*

Moldova *1.55%*

Lithuania *1.46%*

Kyrgyzstan *0.02%*

Latvia *0.99%*

Kazakhstan *0.07%*

Georgia *1.89%*

Estonia *0.56%*

Belarus *4.18%*

Azerbaijan *3.75%*

Armenia *1.33%*

*"Communism" is the term used to describe a **sociopolitical movement** in which the government distributes the country's economical wealth fairly and where citizens work different jobs but are paid and taxed equally—there are no class divisions.*

From Lenin to Gorbachev, communism in the Soviet Union lasted seventy-four years and played a vital role in saving the world from the Nazis, but its political principles were also responsible for the slaughter of up to 50 million of its own citizens, mainly while Stalin was leader from 1924 to 1953.

The Countercultural Revolution_

The movement referred to as **"counterculture"** covers a period from the late 1950s to the early 1970s when the disaffected youth of America, Britain, and other western European countries **rebelled against the establishment**. While the movement didn't lead to any actual changes in government, it did have long-lasting effects on politics. It also led to important developments in many areas of life, from art and fashion to music and technology.

No single event led to the rise of the counterculture, but rather it was a growing feeling that those in power could not be trusted, combined with a rejection of the restraints imposed as a result of postwar shortages.

In the United States, this dissatisfaction manifested itself in the form of protests supporting the **civil rights movement**, opposing the Vietnam War, pushing for a growth in feminism, gay pride, and appeals for free speech.

Across Europe it was students who acted as the front line of the counterculture movement. This reached its height with the **student revolt in Paris in 1968**, the closest any of the activities came to a regime change. Underlying, and possibly weakening, the legitimacy of the movement's aims was the prevalence of drug use, mainly in the form of LSD and marijuana.

At a time when global communication was becoming more accessible and convenient, the world became a melting pot for ideas, so the movement was influenced by figures who would become icons for years to come. The list is wide-ranging and internationally eclectic, and includes Malcolm X, Martin Luther King, the Beatles, Gandhi, Che Guevara, and John F. Kennedy.

Something to Think About . . .

During research into analeptics—drugs that stimulate the central nervous system—LSD-25 was first synthesized in 1938 by Dr. Albert Hoffman in Basel, Switzerland. Hoffman initially discarded it as useless. It was not until five years later that he revisited it and discovered its mind-altering qualities. It then became the drug of the 1960s hippie culture.

Antiwar movement
In 1969 newly elected President Richard Nixon promises to end the Vietnam War, a conflict that had divided America and had continued for many years despite doubts over what it was actually being fought for. It finally ended in 1975.

Cold War
A state of military tension between the United States and the Soviet Union that began in the aftermath of World War II.

Civil rights
On February 21, 1965, African American human-rights activist Malcolm X—a Muslim spokesperson for racial equality in the United States—is assassinated before giving a speech on Afro-American unity.

Social revolution
Between 1963 and 1973, the United States and Britain undergo a massive social transformation with young people rebelling against conservative social norms and questioning the authority of government. The phrase "power to the people" becomes common and the middle of the decade sees the rise of the hippie culture, art-house cinema, and heavy rock music, with the Woodstock festival taking place in 1969.

Nuclear emergency
The Soviet Union has been collaborating with Cuba on building bases within arm's reach of the United States. As a result, the Cuban Missile Crisis of October 1962 is one of the main confrontations between the Soviet Union and United States during the Cold War, causing huge social distress.

Space adventures
In 1961 President John F. Kennedy declares that a manned spacecraft would land on the Moon by the end of the decade. It does, on July 20, 1969.

Sexual revolution
In 1960 the U.S. Food and Drug Administration approves the first female birth-control pill. This aids the radicalization of the previously taboo subject of sex in the Western world, as well as changing social attitudes toward a woman's role in modern society.

Women's rights
Until the 1960s, a woman's place was believed to be in the home, as wife and mother. This changes in 1963 when the Equal Pay Act in the UK breaks down the final legal barrier for a woman's right to work and be paid fairly. By 1968, "women's liberation" has become a household phrase, and the successful breaking down of barriers for equality in the workplace carries on into the 1990s.

Drug culture
With the rise of youth culture and antiauthoritarian behavior, it isn't long before drug use escalates among teenagers. With drugs like LSD and marijuana popular among the new wave of musicians and artists in the United States and Britain, the drug culture expands into other areas of mainstream culture, including fashion and film, with people being encouraged to "tune in, turn on, and drop out."

The Modern Family_

Ever since *Homo sapiens* evolved, humans have lived together in **family units**. The size and function of these units has varied over the centuries, but the basis has remained the same: two parents and their children. If one of the reasons why human beings simply exist at all is to **continue our species' existence**, then the family unit has proved to be a very successful way of achieving this.

Before the industrial revolution in the nineteenth century and mass transportation links, generations of families would all stay in close proximity, creating an extended family unit. As work and industry became concentrated in the **major conurbations**, people had to—or chose to—relocate to find work, and the extended family unit has given way to the simpler **nuclear family**.

When divorce and single parenthood became more common and socially acceptable in the 1960s and 1970s, a new phenomenon arose. It is now common for divorced parents to take their existing family and join it with another so that there is a string of connected **nuclear units**, with siblings and half-siblings stretching across a single generation but with wide age differences. The 1980s and 1990s also saw a doubling in the number of **single-parent families** and a small increase in the number of married or cohabiting couples who chose not to have children. In the early twenty-first century there has also been a surprising shift back to households where children remain living with their parents well into adulthood.

Something to Think About . . .

In a 2002 census taken by the U.S. Census Bureau, 5 billion more people now inhabit the world than in 1800. In fact, in the year 2002 alone, the world gained two people per second—that's 200,000 more people per day and 6.2 million more per month.

Global average household size in 2010 *(in persons)*

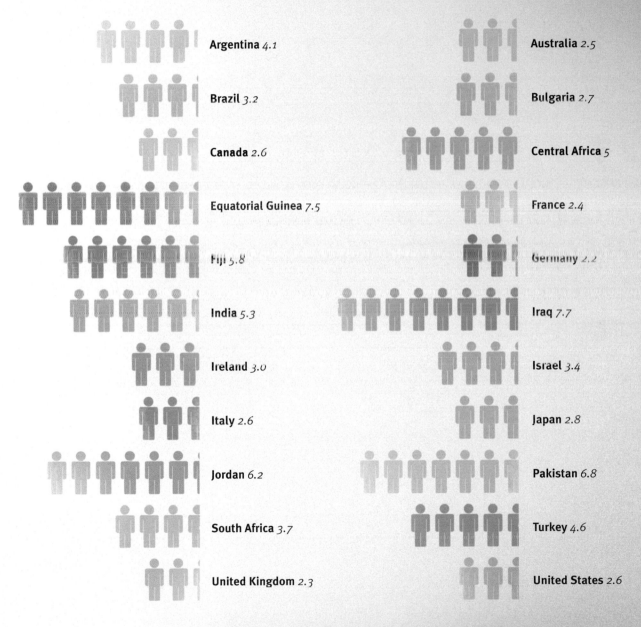

Argentina *4.1*

Brazil *3.2*

Canada *2.6*

Equatorial Guinea *7.5*

Fiji *5.8*

India *5.3*

Ireland *3.0*

Italy *2.6*

Jordan *6.2*

South Africa *3.7*

United Kingdom *2.3*

Australia *2.5*

Bulgaria *2.7*

Central Africa *5*

France *2.4*

Germany *2.2*

Iraq *7.7*

Israel *3.4*

Japan *2.8*

Pakistan *6.8*

Turkey *4.6*

United States *2.6*

Every five minutes, sixty-seven babies are born in the United States, 274 babies are born in China, and 395 babies are born in India.

The World Since 9/11_

The events of **September 11, 2001**, changed the world. When two hijacked commercial aircraft flew into the twin towers of the World Trade Center in New York, a dividing line was drawn in history so that we now think of the time "before 9/11" and "after 9/11" as two separate periods, almost as distinct as BC and AD. The total number of people killed on that day stands at 2,819, a tragedy on a scale that a city had never before suffered in peacetime.

We live in an **economic world**, and an event such as 9/11 will impact destructively upon the global stock markets. Indeed, the **Financial Times and Stock Exchange** (or FTSE)—a share index of the hundred most highly capitalized UK companies listed on the London Stock Exchange—saw an immediate dip following the terror attacks on 9/11, followed by a short spike. What this says about our world is open to debate. Did it affect us at all?

In the aftermath of 9/11, there was a U.S.-led **invasion of Iraq,** where there have been over 100,000 civilian deaths. While this war continues to rage on in the region, the rest of the world continues to turn and go about its business.

This graph shows how various world events have affected the FTSE 100 share index.

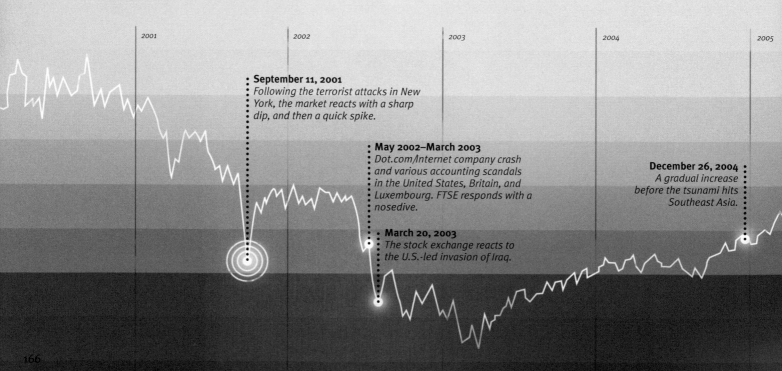

2001   2002   2003   2004   2005

September 11, 2001
Following the terrorist attacks in New York, the market reacts with a sharp dip, and then a quick spike.

May 2002–March 2003
Dot.com/Internet company crash and various accounting scandals in the United States, Britain, and Luxembourg. FTSE responds with a nosedive.

March 20, 2003
The stock exchange reacts to the U.S.-led invasion of Iraq.

December 26, 2004
A gradual increase before the tsunami hits Southeast Asia.

Something to Think About . . .

On October 26, 2001, U.S. president George W. Bush signed into law the U.S. Patriot Act. As an acronym, the individual letters stand for "Uniting and Strengthening America by Providing Appropriate Tools Required to Intercept and Obstruct Terrorism." Immediately after 9/11, the people and government of the United States were united against crimes of terrorism, but since the act has been instigated, it has come under fire for breaching the privacy and civil liberties of many Americans as well as foreigners.

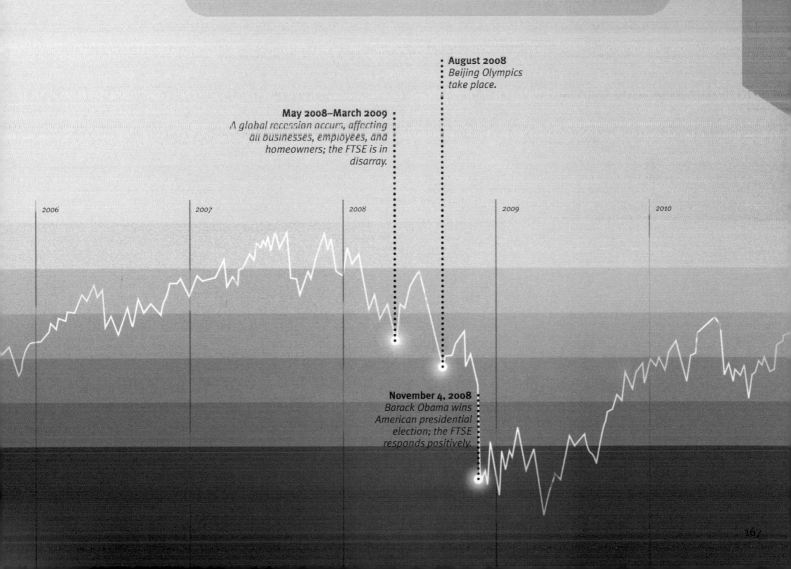

August 2008
Beijing Olympics take place.

May 2008–March 2009
A global recession occurs, affecting all businesses, employees, and homeowners; the FTSE is in disarray.

November 4, 2008
Barack Obama wins American presidential election; the FTSE responds positively.

2006   2007   2008   2009   2010

Chapter 07.0 **Science & Medicine_**

07.1 The Size of Atoms_

Atoms are everywhere and *everything*. You are made up of and surrounded by them. This page contains billions of them, and there are trillions more of them everywhere you look. However, they are very small. So microscopic that you could fit billions of them in the period at the end of this sentence.

Atoms join together to form other things. One of the most well-known examples of this is the combination of an **atom of oxygen** joining up with the **two atoms of hydrogen**. Together these create water—**H_2o**. When atoms combine, they create **molecules**. However, molecules cannot combine randomly because the way they bind together affects what they create—in the same way that sticking four wooden legs, a seat, and a backrest together creates a chair only if assembled correctly.

Something to Think About . . .

A proton's mass is essentially the same as that of a neutron. A proton's mass, however, is 1,840 times greater than the mass of an electron.

*An atom is the basic **chemical building block** of all matter—everything that we see, hear, touch, and smell. Atoms are life.*

*Atoms are made up of **protons** (carrying a positive electric charge), **neutrons** (no electric charge), and **electrons** (carrying a negative electric charge).*

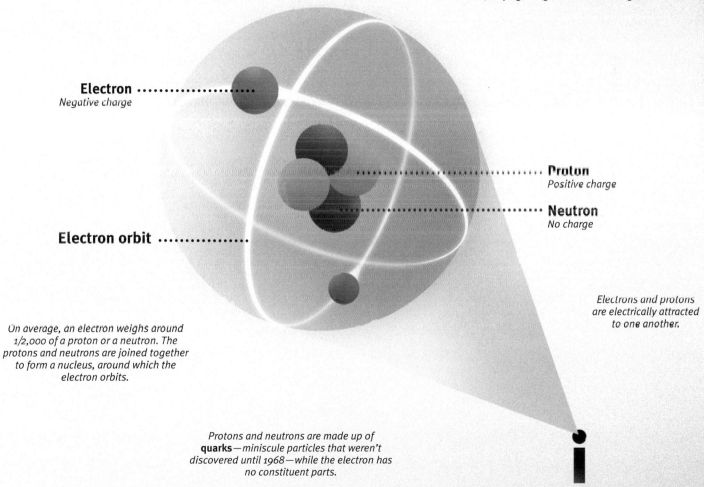

Electron
Negative charge

Proton
Positive charge

Neutron
No charge

Electron orbit

Electrons and protons are electrically attracted to one another.

On average, an electron weighs around 1/2,000 of a proton or a neutron. The protons and neutrons are joined together to form a nucleus, around which the electron orbits.

*Protons and neutrons are made up of **quarks**—miniscule particles that weren't discovered until 1968—while the electron has no constituent parts.*

If a hydrogen atom were 1 inch in diameter, the electron's orbit would be 4,100 feet away!

171

Newton's Gravity_

You can't see it, you can't touch it, but without gravity we'd all be floating around in space. The force of gravity holds us, keeps us on the surface of the Earth, keeps the planet in a stable orbit around the Sun, and generally keeps the universe in order.

Sir Isaac Newton is best known for his (probably apocryphal) observation of **an apple falling from a tree**. Seeing the fruit fall (or not) led him to come up with his **universal law of gravitation**, which he explained in his *Principia* in 1687. The law states, to put it simply, that everything attracts everything else. The strength of the force of attraction can be calculated if you know the objects' masses and the distance between them.

Newton's law remained from when the *Principia* was published until Albert Einstein came along in the early twentieth century. Published in 1915, **Einstein's theory of general relativity** proposed that the warping of space-time caused the apparent attraction of objects. This showed that two objects that one would expect to travel in straight lines without getting closer to one another followed those lines but did become closer, because the straight lines became curved.

Newton's theory and its accompanying equation are simpler and are still used today, but Einstein's theory remains dominant because it explains certain anomalies not covered by Newton.

Something to Think About . . .

In a vacuum, all objects are affected by gravity in the same way. So a tennis ball and a cannonball would, when thrown from the same height, fall to the ground at the same speed.

Gravitational constant $\cdots\cdots$

Mass of first object

Gravitational force $\cdots\cdots$

Mass of second object

$$F = \frac{G m_1 m_2}{r^2}$$

Distance between the two objects

07.3 The Periodic Table of Elements_

The chemical elements are the **building blocks** of everything we see around us. The elements themselves cannot be broken down any further, and everything we know about our lives and the universe is built from them. The atoms that form each element are attributed to an **atomic number** based on the **number of protons in the atom's nucleus.**

Russian chemist Dmitry Mendeleyev is credited with creating the periodic table in 1869. Mendeleyev placed the elements in rows in order of their atomic number and started a new row when an element's properties were repeated, hence the term "periodic." Looking at the columns of the table enables the grouping of elements by their properties. This arrangement was Mendeleyev's first groundbreaking discovery. His second was when he realized that the table had some gaps and that these gaps represented elements that had not yet been discovered. When he first drew up the table, there were only sixty-five known elements. There are now 118.

In addition to its atomic number, each element has a corresponding symbol (for instance, **hydrogen** is H and **tin** is Sn) and an atomic mass. The table is used in all aspects of science and is an invaluable resource. Because elements in the same groups behave and react similarly, it allows scientists to predict the reaction even of unknown elements.

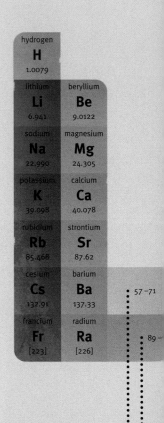

Something to Think About . . .

Element 117 is currently called Ununseptium (Latin for the number 117). Its discovery has not yet been confirmed, but the gap in the table shows that there *must* be something there.

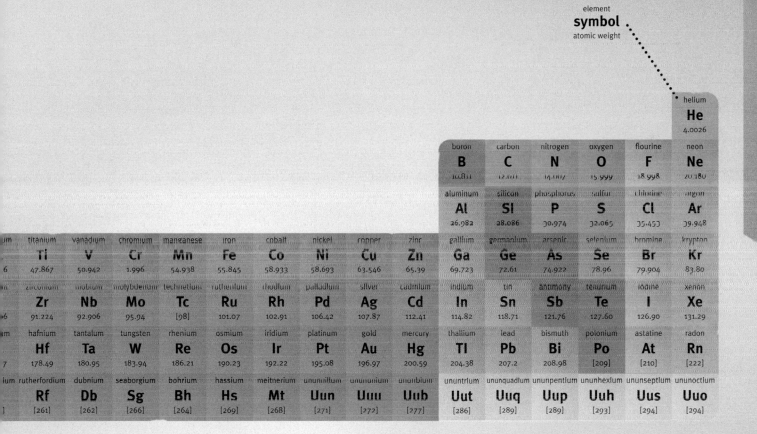

			element
			symbol
			atomic weight

					helium
					He
					4.0026

boron	carbon	nitrogen	oxygen	flourine	neon
B	**C**	**N**	**O**	**F**	**Ne**
10.811	12.011	14.007	15.999	18.998	20.180

aluminum	silicon	phosphorus	sulfur	chlorine	argon
Al	**Si**	**P**	**S**	**Cl**	**Ar**
26.982	28.086	30.974	32.065	35.453	39.948

titanium	vanadium	chromium	manganese	iron	cobalt	nickel	copper	zinc	gallium	germanium	arsenic	selenium	bromine	krypton
Ti	**V**	**Cr**	**Mn**	**Fe**	**Co**	**Ni**	**Cu**	**Zn**	**Ga**	**Ge**	**As**	**Se**	**Br**	**Kr**
47.867	50.942	1.996	54.938	55.845	58.933	58.693	63.546	65.39	69.723	72.61	74.922	78.96	79.904	83.80

zirconium	niobium	molybdenum	technetium	ruthenium	rhodium	palladium	silver	cadmium	indium	tin	antimony	tellurium	iodine	xenon
Zr	**Nb**	**Mo**	**Tc**	**Ru**	**Rh**	**Pd**	**Ag**	**Cd**	**In**	**Sn**	**Sb**	**Te**	**I**	**Xe**
91.224	92.906	95.94	[98]	101.07	102.91	106.42	107.87	112.41	114.82	118.71	121.76	127.60	126.90	131.29

hafnium	tantalum	tungsten	rhenium	osmium	iridium	platinum	gold	mercury	thallium	lead	bismuth	polonium	astatine	radon
Hf	**Ta**	**W**	**Re**	**Os**	**Ir**	**Pt**	**Au**	**Hg**	**Tl**	**Pb**	**Bi**	**Po**	**At**	**Rn**
178.49	180.95	183.94	186.21	190.23	192.22	195.08	196.97	200.59	204.38	207.2	208.98	[209]	[210]	[222]

rutherfordium	dubnium	seaborgium	bohrium	hassium	meitnerium	ununillium	unununium	ununbium	ununtrium	ununquadium	ununpentium	ununhexium	ununseptium	ununoctium
Rf	**Db**	**Sg**	**Bh**	**Hs**	**Mt**	**Uun**	**Uuu**	**Uub**	**Uut**	**Uuq**	**Uup**	**Uuh**	**Uus**	**Uuo**
[261]	[262]	[266]	[264]	[269]	[268]	[271]	[272]	[277]	[286]	[289]	[289]	[293]	[294]	[294]

lanthanum	cerium	praseo-dymium	neodymium	promethium	samarium	europium	gadolinium	terbium	dysprosium	holmium	erbium	thulium	ytterbium
La	**Ce**	**Pr**	**Nd**	**Pm**	**Sm**	**Eu**	**Gd**	**Tb**	**Dy**	**Ho**	**Er**	**Tm**	**Yb**
138.91	140.12	140.91	144.24	[145]	150.36	151.96	157.25	158.93	162.50	164.93	167.26	168.93	173.04

actinium	thorium	protactinium	uranium	neptunium	plutonium	americium	curium	berkelium	californium	einsteinium	fermium	mendelevium	nobelium
Ac	**Th**	**Pa**	**U**	**Np**	**Pu**	**Am**	**Cm**	**Bk**	**Cf**	**Es**	**Fm**	**Md**	**No**
[227]	232.04	231.04	238.03	[237]	[244]	[243]	[247]	[247]	888	[252]	[257]	[258]	[259]

- ■ *Alkali metals*
- ■ *Alkaline earth metals*
- ■ *Lanthanides*
- ■ *Actinides*
- ■ *Transition elements*
- ■ *Poor metals*
- ■ *Metalloids*
- ■ *Other nonmetals*
- ■ *Halogens*
- ■ *Noble gases*
- ■ *Unknown chemical properties*

Equations You Need to Know_

All the sciences rely on mathematics to make sense of the world, and everything we do can be illustrated or explained using mathematics. Whether it is figuring out how long we will have to wait for the next bus or predicting when an asteroid may hit Earth, **mathematics is vital**.

Early mathematics was used purely to deal with the everyday elements of life such as commerce and farming, but once it was realized that mathematics could be used to describe the world we live in, and even predict outcomes, its **possibilities became infinite**. There is a beauty and simplicity to mathematics that does not exist in the other sciences. The **golden ratio** is an example of mathematics crossing over into another discipline and setting a standard for it.

The golden ratio is used in art all the time: it states that a line with a total length $a + b$ is to the length of the longer segment a as the length of a is to the length of the shorter segment b. This ratio is seen in many classic works of art, such as the *Mona Lisa*. The ratio of the height of her face to the width is the golden ratio, as is her forehead's width and height, as displayed in the ratio below:

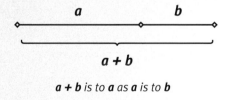

a + b is to **a** as **a** is to **b**

Something to Think About . . .

The number zero (0) was identified as early as the fifth century by mathematicians in India. Zero was used repeatedly when looking at stars and gauging distances. Before zero spread across the world, Europeans used Roman numerals to do calculations, although this made it difficult because Roman numerals use symbols, and have obvious limitations when dealing with lots of numbers.

Equation 1
Pi

C: circumference of a circle

$$\pi = \frac{C}{d}$$

π: Pi

d: diameter of a circle

Equation 2
Albert Einstein's theory of general relativity

$$E = mc^2$$

E: energy

m: mass

c: the speed of light

Equation 3
Sir Isaac Newton's second law of mechanics

$$F = ma$$

F: force

m: mass

a: acceleration

Equation 4
Pythagorean theorem

$$a^2 + b^2 = c^2$$

a and b: the two shortest sides of a right triangle

c: the long side

Equation 5
Repaying your mortgage

C: loan amount

N: number of months

$$P = \frac{Cr(1+r)^N}{(1+r)^N - 1}$$

P: monthly payment

r: monthly interest (1/12 of annual rate)

Equation 6
Area of a circle

$$A = \pi r^2$$

A: area

π: Pi

r: radius

07.5 How Electricity Works_

Around the **nucleus** of every atom there are **electrons** that move around it. When the electrons are given "energy" by a power source, they jump from one atom to the next. This movement is an **electric current**. It is this current, or **movement of electrons**, that makes electrical objects work. The vital element that electricity needs is a completed circuit. When we flick a light switch, we are completing a circuit that allows the electrons to move, and this is what makes the bulb light up.

In the wire that makes up most of the circuit, the electrons can move freely, without much resistance, like water through a wide pipe, but when they reach the lightbulb and its filament—the part that lights up—the **resistance is high**, as though the pipe is too narrow. It is this resistance, and the strain it puts on the movement of the electrons, that **heats up the filament** and makes the bulb glow.

Something to Think About . . .

Italian physicist Alessandro Volta is credited with inventing the first electric battery in 1800, but this discovery only came about thanks indirectly to experiments carried out on frogs' legs in 1791 by Luigi Galvani, who noticed that their muscles twitched when an electric charge was introduced.

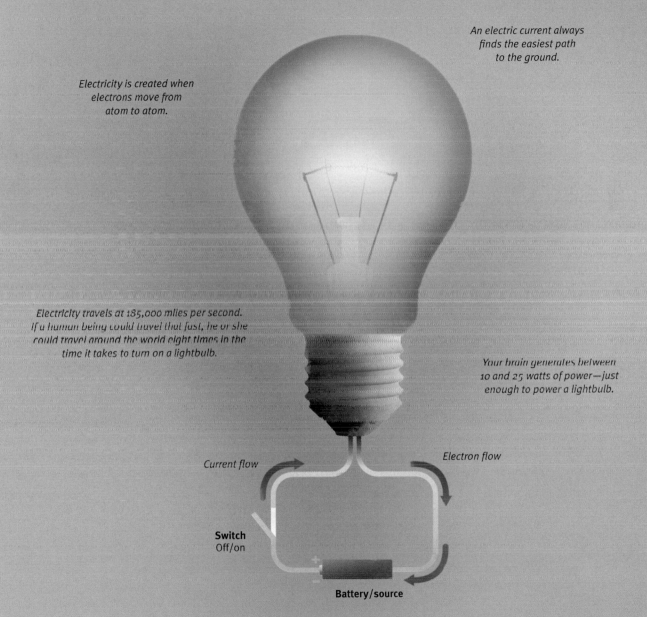

An electric current always finds the easiest path to the ground.

Electricity is created when electrons move from atom to atom.

Electricity travels at 185,000 miles per second. If a human being could travel that fast, he or she could travel around the world eight times in the time it takes to turn on a lightbulb.

Your brain generates between 10 and 25 watts of power—just enough to power a lightbulb.

Current flow

Electron flow

Switch
Off/on

Battery/source

A power source can be either direct current or alternating current. A battery is an example of the former, and the charge is caused by a chemical reaction. A power station creates alternating current due to the movement of a magnet within a copper coil.

The Inside Life of Bacteria_

The bacteria that exist on and around us today began their evolution not long after Earth came into existence. Bacteria are **single-celled organisms** and have the basic structure that would have been found in the very first organisms, from which everything eventually evolved. In essence, they were the **first life-forms** to develop on Earth.

Bacteria have a reputation for being harmful. In fact, there are more **helpful bacteria** types than harmful types. For instance, the bacteria located in the human stomach are vital for digestion, producing vitamins, and stimulating the immune system.

Bacterial infection develops when the bacteria gain access to the body's tissue. The site of access is generally the mouth, nose, and eyes, but they can also enter via wounds. These infections can, if left to run their course, cause plagues and **death on a large scale** (such as the bubonic plague, which killed up to 77 million people between 1348 and 1350 in Europe). The development of antibacterial drugs, or **antibiotics**, has helped us to reduce these epidemic incidents. Before antibiotics were readily available, chemist Louis Pasteur discovered in 1864 that the process of boiling kills all known bacteria, hence the term **pasteurization**.

Something to Think About . . .

The first microbiologist, Dutchman Antony van Leeuwenhoek, was also the first person to "see" bacteria. He pioneered high-powered microscopes to look at, among many other things, pond water, in which he first saw bacteria.

The structure of a bacterial cell

*Bacteria are split into two groups: **bacteria** and **cyanobacteria**. Cyanobacteria are responsible for the creation of our oxygen-rich atmosphere.*

*Bacteria come in three shapes: **sphere** (coccus), **rod** (bacillus), and **spiral** (spirillum).*

Capsule

Cell wall

Plasma membrane

Bacteria can survive and thrive at a wide range of temperatures.

Ribosomes

Cytoplasm

Nucleoid

Pili

Antibiotics—such as the most common, penicillin—interfere with the insides of a bacterial cell and prevent it from multiplying.

Bacterial flagellum

Bacteria are roughly 1,000 nanometers in size. A nanometer is a millionth of a millimeter.

There are more bacterial cells in our bodies than there are human cells. There are even more bacterial cells in one person's body than there are people on the planet!

The Rules of Magnetic Attraction_

A magnet is an object or material that produces a **magnetic field**. The planet Earth is a magnet. All magnets have a north pole and a south pole. The rule of magnetism is: unlike poles **attract,** like poles **repel**.

The magnetic field is created by the **movement of electrons** within the magnet. The fact that the magnetism comes from this action also links magnets to electricity, in what we call **electromagnetism**. They are two sides of the same coin.

There are two types of magnets: **permanent magnets** and **electromagnets**. In the former, the magnetic field is fixed and is always in operation. In an electromagnet, the magnetic field is only operational when the current is flowing. These different properties mean that different jobs are best performed by one type or the other. The magnet that holds notes to your fridge is an example of a permanent magnet. Electromagnets are found in most machines that we use regularly, such as cars, stereos, televisions, and computers.

When an **electric current** flows along a wire, a magnetic field is created, and when you spin a magnet within a wire coil, you get an electric current. Knowing this—and a little about electrons (which orbit around the nucleus of an atom)—explains how a magnetic field can be created without an apparent electric current.

Something to Think About . . .

In Shanghai, China, a train called a maglev uses magnetic levitation—the process by which magnets are used to make objects float—to transport people around. The maglev train can travel, on average, around 160 miles per hour—much faster than a conventional train on a track.

Earth's magnetic power comes from its liquid center, which makes it a massive electromagnet.

The magnetic pull is always strongest at the poles.

Magnetic attraction works at great distances, and even in a vacuum such as outer space.

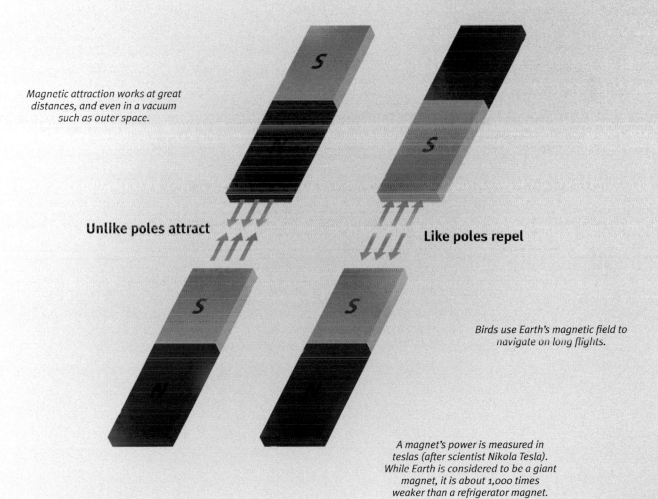

Unlike poles attract

Like poles repel

Birds use Earth's magnetic field to navigate on long flights.

A magnet's power is measured in teslas (after scientist Nikola Tesla). While Earth is considered to be a giant magnet, it is about 1,000 times weaker than a refrigerator magnet.

There are not many materials that have magnetic properties. Iron is a natural magnetic metal; other magnetic metals include nickel and cobalt.

07.8 The Unique History of Measurement_

Three of the main dimensions that we measure are **distance**, **weight**, and **time**. They are all made up of finite units, and these units have become standardized around the world. One **second** in Boston, England, is the same length of time as one second in Boston, Massachusetts. One **kilogram** in Madrid is the same as one kilogram in Manchester, and one **meter** is the same on Long Island as it is in Littlehampton. This is vital, so that around the globe when you order four kilograms of flour to be delivered in three days, the people you are ordering from know exactly what you mean.

Today's **metric system** owes much to the French Revolution of 1789–99 and King Louis XVI. The French monarch ordered that a **new system of measurement** be developed to provide something more **universally applicable** than what had previously been used.

In the United States, however, most people rely on measurements derived from the **imperial system**, which was introduced in Britain in 1824 but was later replaced by the metric system across much of the world.

Something to Think About . . .

Every 30 million years, even the world's most accurate clocks, such as NIST-F1 at the American National Institute of Standards and Technology in Maryland, will gain or lose one second.

**Comparing the origin of measurements
to how they are calculated now**

Historic

New

This was based on the apparent movement of the Sun around the Earth. A solar day was divided by 24 (into hours); these were divided by 60 (into minutes), and each minute was further divided by 60 to give the length of a second.

A second

Since 1967, a second has been defined as the duration of 9,192,631,770 periods of the radiation corresponding to the transition between the two hyperfine levels of the ground state of the cesium 133 atom.

A meter was originally defined as 1/10,000,000 of the distance from the North Pole to the equator.

A meter

A meter is the length of the path traveled by light in a vacuum during a time interval of 1/299,792,458 of a second. The word "meter" was introduced into the English language in 1797.

Three barleycorns; after 1606, barleycorns were used because they are uniform in length: 8 millimeters.

An inch

2.54 centimeters

The mass of a liter of water at 0°C.

A kilogram

Equal to the mass of the international prototype of the kilogram, which is a cylinder made of an alloy for which the mass fraction of platinum is 90 percent and the mass fraction of iridium is 10 percent.

7,200 wheat grains

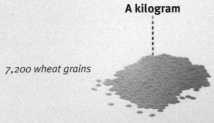

A pound

0.45359237 kilograms

The Medical Trade_

When we are ill and want to get better, we take medicine. The word "medicine" covers a multitude of treatments, but they all fall into three different areas in terms of how they work.

- **Replacing a deficiency:** *supplement*
- **Killing an intruder:** *assassin*
- **Changing the behavior of the cells:** *modifier*

Supplement
Rickets, a softening of the bones that can lead to fractures and deformity, is an example of a deficiency disease and can be treated with a combination of vitamin D, calcium, and sunlight.

Assassin
Bacterial infections are a major cause of illness, and penicillin is probably the most well-known and commonly used treatment. Penicillin was discovered by accident in 1928 by Alexander Fleming. At its most basic level, penicillin works by breaking down the cell walls of bacteria.

Modifier
Ibuprofen, like most modifiers, does not actually cure you of the illness, but it will relieve the symptoms, often completely. By inhibiting cyclooxygenase, an enzyme responsible for producing pain signals, ibuprofen effectively tricks the body into thinking it is not in pain.

In addition to the three methods of operation, it is important to consider the delivery method. Drugs are carried around the body by the blood, and thus the speed of absorption into the blood will affect a treatment's efficiency.

- **Intravenous:** *introduced directly into the blood*
- **Intramuscular:** *introduced directly into a muscle*
- **Subcutaneous:** *introduced just under the skin*
- **Rectal:** *introduced through the bowel*
- **Oral:** *taken by swallowing*

The choice depends on the type of medicine, the illness involved, and the speed and period of delivery required. It might seem that one would always want delivery to be as quick as possible, but some treatments need a slow, long release, such as insulin for diabetes.

Something to Think About . . .

Nonprescription drugs such as alcohol, caffeine, and nicotine are still the most abused drugs in the world. Over 450 million cups of coffee are consumed in the United States each day (that's 1.5 cups for every man, woman, and child), and a 10-gram dose of caffeine is considered lethal. One cup of coffee contains about 100 milligrams of caffeine.

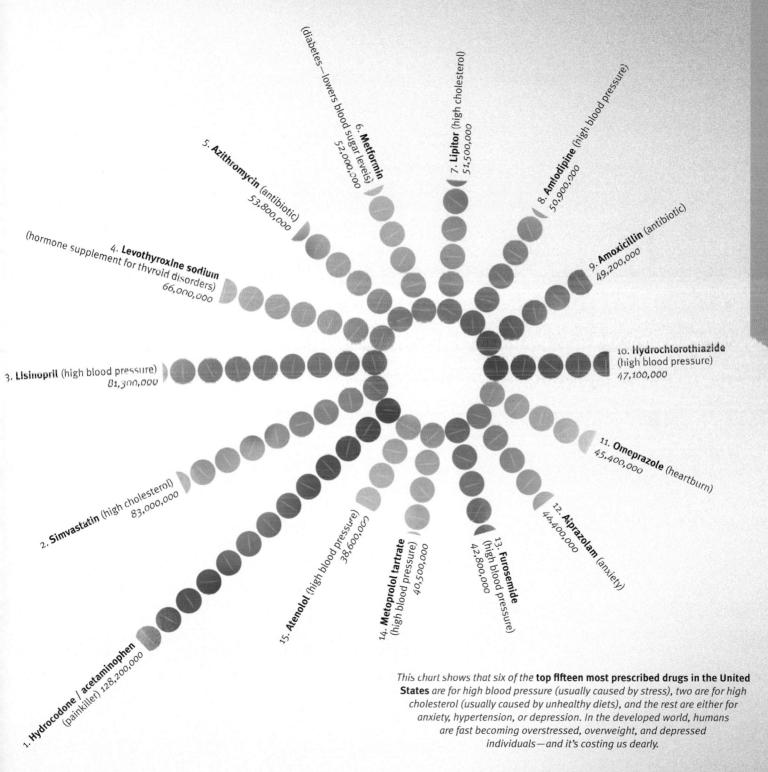

5. **Azithromycin** (antibiotic)
53,800,000

6. **Metformin**
(diabetes—lowers blood sugar levels)
52,000,000

7. **Lipitor** (high cholesterol)
51,500,000

8. **Amlodipine** (high blood pressure)
50,900,000

4. **Levothyroxine sodium**
(hormone supplement for thyroid disorders)
66,000,000

9. **Amoxicillin** (antibiotic)
49,200,000

3. **Lisinopril** (high blood pressure)
81,300,000

10. **Hydrochlorothiazide**
(high blood pressure)
47,100,000

11. **Omeprazole** (heartburn)
45,400,000

2. **Simvastatin** (high cholesterol)
83,000,000

12. **Alprazolam** (anxiety)
44,400,000

15. **Atenolol** (high blood pressure)
38,600,000

14. **Metoprolol tartrate**
(high blood pressure)
40,500,000

13. **Furosemide**
(high blood pressure)
42,800,000

1. **Hydrocodone / acetaminophen**
(painkiller) 128,200,000

This chart shows that six of the **top fifteen most prescribed drugs in the United States** are for high blood pressure (usually caused by stress), two are for high cholesterol (usually caused by unhealthy diets), and the rest are either for anxiety, hypertension, or depression. In the developed world, humans are fast becoming overstressed, overweight, and depressed individuals—and it's costing us dearly.

07.10 **What's Killing Us?**

There are many ways for human beings to die, and as we have evolved we have learned how to avoid it for longer. It is true to say that because of the way we live now, the things that kill us—or at least make us ill—have changed as well. It is even possible to prove that we are now being brought down by diseases that previously would not have affected us, simply because we are living longer and giving the diseases more opportunities to attack.

The World Health Organization, when looking at the causes of death, has three main categories: (1) **noncommunicable conditions** (responsible for 58.65 percent of deaths); (2) **communicable diseases**, maternal and perinatal conditions, and nutritional deficiencies (32.31 percent); and (3) **injuries** (9.04 percent).

Worldwide, the single biggest killer is **cardiovascular disease**, which accounts for nearly 30 percent of deaths. Cancer in all its various forms takes 12.46 percent, and HIV/AIDS is responsible for just over 5 percent. Amazingly, road traffic accidents kill over 2 percent but war is responsible for only 0.3 percent, while intentional self-inflicted injuries cause 1.53 percent of deaths.

The major difference in the developed world between now and the nineteenth century was the **discovery of antibiotics**, especially penicillin. During the nineteenth century, bacterial disease was rife. The top killers in those days were pneumonia, tuberculosis, diphtheria, and typhoid.

Something to Think About . . .

Even if disease doesn't kill us, humans still age and die. This aging is due to the deterioration of a protective cap on our chromosomes. In 2010 researchers at Harvard University reversed the signs of aging in mice by manipulating this cap. Human testing may begin soon.

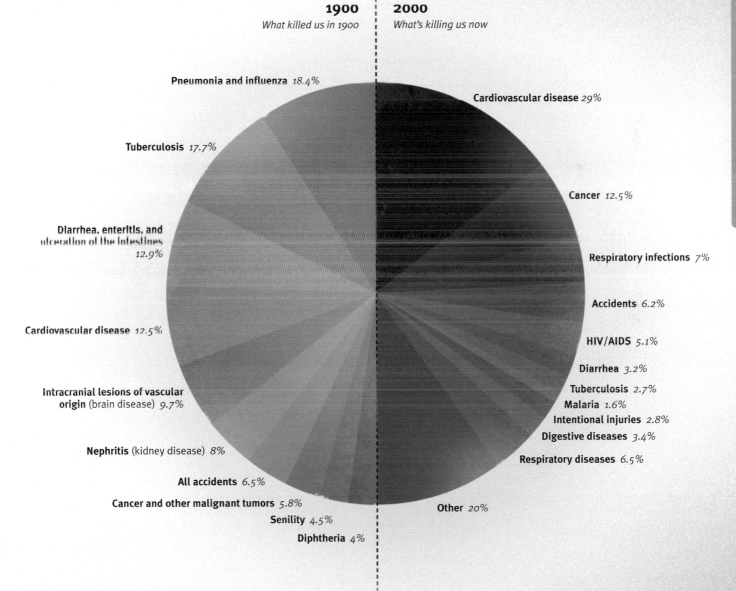

1900
What killed us in 1900

2000
What's killing us now

Pneumonia and influenza *18.4%*

Tuberculosis *17.7%*

Diarrhea, enteritis, and ulceration of the intestines *12.9%*

Cardiovascular disease *12.5%*

Intracranial lesions of vascular origin (brain disease) *9.7%*

Nephritis (kidney disease) *8%*

All accidents *6.5%*

Cancer and other malignant tumors *5.8%*

Senility *4.5%*

Diphtheria *4%*

Cardiovascular disease *29%*

Cancer *12.5%*

Respiratory infections *7%*

Accidents *6.2%*

HIV/AIDS *5.1%*

Diarrhea *3.2%*

Tuberculosis *2.7%*

Malaria *1.6%*

Intentional injuries *2.8%*

Digestive diseases *3.4%*

Respiratory diseases *6.5%*

Other *20%*

(Figures shown are for the United States.)

The Speed of Speed_

The comic-book superhero Superman can travel faster than a speeding bullet—that is indeed exceptionally quick. But **nothing is faster than the speed of light**. For a long time, until the mid-seventeenth century, most people thought that light traveled instantaneously.

In 1676 Danish astronomer Ole Romer first noticed that light traveled at a **finite speed**. In observing the lunar eclipses of Jupiter, he realized that they happened earlier than expected when Earth was closer to Jupiter. The only explanation for this was that the light took less time to reach us and therefore could not be instantaneous.

One of the important things to note about the speed of light is that its **speed is constant**. It does not vary regardless of the source, be it the light in your fridge or the most expensive military laser. The constancy and rapidity of the speed of light is useful for measuring objects that are great distances away from Earth. It is common scientific practice to refer to distances in space not by the distance in miles but by how many years it takes light to reach the object; a **light-year** is the distance light travels in one year.

The speed of light is denoted as c and is a vital component in the formulation of **Einstein's theory of special relativity**.

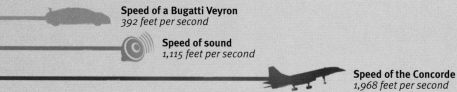

Speed of a Bugatti Veyron
392 feet per second

Speed of sound
1,115 feet per second

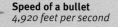

Speed of the Concorde
1,968 feet per second

Speed of a bullet
4,920 feet per second

Speed of a cheetah
106 feet per second

Speed of top male sprinter
34 feet per second

0

Something to Think About . . .

Light travels at 671 million miles per hour. To us, that appears instantaneous. In the context of space, it's rather slow. If you were to have a conversation with an astronaut on Mars, it would take the radio signals—traveling at the speed of light— 42 minutes to reach Earth.

Speed of light
983,319,262 feet per second

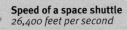

Speed of a space shuttle
26,400 feet per second

1 second

Science and Medicine's Finest Hours_

It is obvious, from the world we see around us everyday, that there have been many **amazing advances** in the worlds of science and medicine since human beings have been able to think independently. It is often the case, however, that the scientists, mathematicians, and doctors we associate with a particular development in these fields were not necessarily the first to make that discovery. They were just the best at communicating their finds.

What is not in doubt is that any new discovery in a field makes development that much easier. It is this development that explains the exponential growth in **the speed of human advancement and achievement**. This growth can be described using the **Fibonacci sequence**, explained in 1202 by Leonardo of Pisa.

580 BC
Pythagoras is born in Samos, Greece.

1749
The father of immunology, Edward Jenner, is born in England.

1804
First surgery under anesthetic performed by Japanese surgeon

460 BC
Hippocrates, the father of medicine, is born in Kos, Greece.

AD 1202
Leonardo of Pisa posits the Fibonacci sequence.

1543
Polish astronomer Nicolaus Copernicus proposes a heliocentric view of the solar system.

1687
Isaac Newton publishes Philosophiae Naturalis Principia Mathematica.

1802
British scientist John Dalton discovers the atom.

Something to Think About . . .

The Fibonacci sequence (in which each number is the sum of the previous two numbers: 0, 1, 1, 2, 3, 5, 8, 13, 21, 34, 55, 89, etc.), while a mathematical construct, is often found in nature. One example is the spiral on a snail's shell.

1818
Dr. James Blundell performs the first successful blood transfusion in London.

1842
American physician Crawford Long uses ether as a general anesthetic.

1850s–60s
Louis Pasteur (France) and Robert Koch (Prussia) establish the germ theory of disease.

1860
Florence Nightingale establishes a training school for nurses.

1897
Aspirin, the wonder drug, is developed in Germany by chemist Felix Hoffmann.

1928
Penicillin is discovered by Scottish biologist Alexander Fleming.

1967
First heart transplant performed by South African heart surgeon Christiaan Barnard.

1983
HIV/AIDS virus is identified.

2010
First full face transplant performed in Spain.

1821
British mathematician and inventor Charles Babbage designs the first computer, Difference Engine 1.

1859
Charles Darwin publishes On the Origin of Species.

1895
Guglielmo Marconi sends a radio signal over 1 mile.

1945
First atomic explosion takes place in New Mexico.

1953
DNA modeled by Francis Crick and James Watson.

1961
Russian cosmonaut Yury Gagarin becomes the first man in space.

1990
Hubble Space Telescope is launched.

Chapter 08.0 Technology & Communications_

08.1 The Science of Progress_

One of the things that distinguishes humans from all other animals on the planet is our ability to invent things. This is a by-product of the **development and evolution** of our brains over time, but also a result of the fact that we are never really satisfied with what we've got.

People often say that **modern-day innovations** and appliances are the "greatest invention since sliced bread." Well, sliced bread, or rather a machine to slice loaves and wrap them in wax paper, was invented in 1928. When it arrived, it led to a massive increase in the consumption of bread, mainly because it was so easy to have just "one more slice." This had not been the original motivation for the invention, and is certainly not the only unexpected consequence of a new discovery or creation. Humanity's **first great discovery**, fire, was initially used merely for warmth, but when it began to be used to cook the meat of dead animals, it had the unforeseen effect of speeding up human evolution.

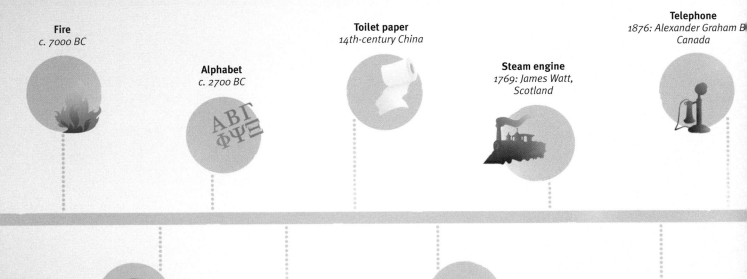

Fire
c. 7000 BC

Alphabet
c. 2700 BC

Toilet paper
14th-century China

Steam engine
1769: James Watt,
Scotland

Telephone
1876: Alexander Graham B
Canada

Wheel
3200 BC

Clock
1090: Su Song,
China

Printing press
1440: Johannes Gutenberg,
Germany

Electricity
1831: Michael Faraday,
England

Something to Think About . . .

The timeline, the idea of displaying simple chronological events graphically, was invented by a Swiss mathematician named Leonhard Euler (1707–83).

Television
1925: John Logie Baird,
Scotland

World Wide Web (Internet)
1989: Tim Berners Lee,
England

Powered flight
1903: Orville and Wilbur Wright,
United States

Computer
1936: Alan Turing,
England

Automobile
1889: Gottlieb Daimler,
Germany

Sliced bread
1928: Otto Frederick Rohwedder,
United States

Electric washing machine
1906 (disputed)

Mobile phone
1973: Martin Cooper (Motorola),
United States

The Evolution of Transportation_

The most important invention since the wheel is a coveted title. It is no secret that the invention of the wheel changed life as we knew it forever. On an average day in the twenty-first century, our **reliance on the wheel** is almost absolute.

The wheel, as a circle and thus a **symbol of renewal and rebirth**, is in itself a powerful metaphor for how this device has helped us survive and flourish. The utilization of this shape as a means of transporting materials, possessions, and ourselves has allowed us to conquer the Earth.

The first wheel was really not a wheel at all but hundreds of wheels all stuck together—more commonly known as a log or tree trunk. By placing a series of trunks under a heavy object, it was possible to move it much more easily than by merely pushing it along the ground. The jump from this to using a slice, or thin cross-section, of a tree was the moment when the first wheel came into existence. The addition of a central axle around which the wheel could move came next. This step, which probably came around 3,000 years ago, was in effect the last development of the wheel.

c. 4000 BC
A series of logs are rolled together; this is how the Egyptians transported the stone that built the Great Pyramids.

c. 3807 BC
Europe's first wooden footpath, the Sweet Track, is built near Glastonbury, England.

c. 3500 BC
Wooden log rafts with oars— or riverboats—are used.

c. 3200 BC
Wheels with axles are produced.

c. 3000 BC
Mesopotamian war chariot appears.

c. 2000 BC
Horses are trained to pull carts.

312 BC
Romans lay down the first paved road and call it the Appian Way.

c. 234–181 BC
The wheelbarrow is invented.

AD 700
Triangular, or lateen, sails are invented, possibly in Egypt.

770
Horseshoes are fitted to improve transportation by horses.

852
The earliest form of parachute is invented.

1266
Compasses first appear in China.

1662
Frenchman Blaise Pascal invents the horse-drawn coach.

1801
Richard Trevithick demonstrates his steam train.

Something to Think About . . .

The Aerostat Reveillon, the first hot-air balloon, was launched on September 19, 1783, by a scientist named Jean Francois Pilatre de Rozier. Onboard passengers were a cockerel, a duck, and a sheep. The first manned hot-air balloon ride took place on November 21, 1783, when Joseph and Etienne Montgolfier took off from Paris. They were in the air for twenty minutes—five minutes longer than their animal counterparts.

1817
German Baron Karl von Drais invents a running bike called the Draisine.

1825
The first public passenger railway, the Stockton and Darlington, opens in northeast England.

1867
The motorcycle is invented.

1870s
James Starley's penny-farthing is invented.

1885
John Kemp Starley invents the safety bicycle—with chain.

1885
Karl Benz builds a practical automobile—the world's first.

1888
John Boyd Dunlop builds the first pneumatic tire.

1903
Orville and Wilbur Wright pilot the first powered aircraft.

1919
The first daily passenger flight from London to Paris.

1947
American Chuck Yeager makes the first supersonic jet flight.

1964
The Japanese invent the bullet train.

1969
First manned spacecraft lands on the Moon.

1970
First jumbo jet takes to the skies.

1981
NASA launches its first space shuttle.

2001
The personal, two-wheeled electric Segway is introduced.

08.3 **The History of the Printed Word_**

The earliest method of printing was produced by carving into wood and then transferring the image to paper by inking the wood. This was very time-consuming and complicated, as whatever was being printed had to be carved in reverse.

The major leap forward came with the production of individual blocks for each letter of the alphabet and the construction of a frame into which these could be placed—this was the **printing press**. While there have been improvements since Johannes Gutenberg invented his printing press in the fifteenth century, the processes used now are essentially the same except everything is done by computers.

Advances in printing technology were vital in the **dissemination of information and ideas**. In dictatorial regimes where ideas printed in books go against the ideology of the current rulers (and where they do not encourage free speech), freedom of expression via the printed word can be a powerful weapon. If it is true that the pen is mightier than the sword, it cannot be denied that **the printing press is mightier than the pen**.

Printing press

1041
In China, Bi Sheng introduces printing using **carved wooden blocks** *covered in ink to transfer text and images to paper.*

1241
Koreans **use metal movable type** *to print books.*

1309
Paper first made by Europeans.

1338
In France, the first paper mill opens.

1430
Intaglio printing *first used.*

1476
In England, **William Caxton** *uses a Gutenberg printing press.*

1501
Italic type *is first used.*

Printed word

AD 868
Diamond Sutra: *The world's first printed book, or the earliest dated printed book found so far.*

1543
Nicolaus Copernicus publishes his **Heavenly Spheres.**

1570
Beware the Cat *by William Baldwin—the first novel in English.*

1605
Relation—*the first weekly newspaper printed in Strasbourg by Johan Carolus.*

1611
King James Bible *published.*

Something to Think About . . .

Louis Braille's six-dot writing system evolved from the tactile *ecriture nocturne* (night writing) code invented by Charles Barbier de la Serre. This code was used to send military messages that could be read on the battlefield at night without light.

1623
William Shakespeare's First Folio — *a collected edition of all his plays. Without this, there would be no Shakespeare today.*

1755
Samuel Johnson publishes the first dictionary.

1785
The Times *(as the Daily Universal Register) is first printed. Oldest national paper in the world.*

1796
Lithography — *a type of printing using a stone or metal plate — is invented by Alois Senefelder.*

1824
*French teenager **Louis Braille**, aged 15, invents the six-dot system that now bears his name.*

1903
*American Ira Washington Rubel accidentally invents **offset printing** when he forgets to put the paper into the press and the ink goes onto the rubber cylinder. When he then inserts the paper, the resulting image on the paper is clearer.*

1920 *(U.S.)*, **1921** *(UK)*
The Mysterious Affair at Styles — *Agatha Christie's first book published.*

1925
Mein Kampf — *Adolf Hitler's autobiography.*

1927
The International Federation of Library Associations and Institutions is founded — they oversee the cataloging of all published books.

1932
*Albatross Books in Germany is credited with creating **the first mass-market paperback books.***

1960
To Kill a Mockingbird by Harper Lee — *regarded as one of the best novels of all time.*

1988
Professor Stephen Hawking publishes **A Brief History of Time** — *a vital and popular book on the history of the universe.*

1995
Web site Amazon.com begins selling books.

1997
Harry Potter and the Philosopher's Stone by *J. K. Rowling released in the UK — only 500 copies in first print run; released in the U.S. in 1998 as Harry Potter and the Sorcerer's Stone.*

1998
Softbook releases the first e-book reader.

2005
The Girl with the Dragon Tattoo by *Stieg Larsson — one of the most popular books of the decade.*

2007
*Amazon releases its first-generation digital **e-book reader**, the Kindle.*

2010
A wide range of e-book readers enter the market.

The History of Communication_

The ancient history of communication is difficult to document because we are limited to what has survived through the ages. While we can make solid assumptions based on **cave drawings**, for instance, we can only guess at how verbal communication developed. Regarding other forms of communication, some researchers believe that information may have been passed on using something as simple as a piece of string with knots in it; however, it is impossible to know for sure because there are no surviving examples to study.

Communication and its evolution can be split into two areas: **oral and visual**. The former developed from basic animal noises, used as warnings or soothing sounds. As we started to walk on two feet, and as our vocal chords changed shape, we were able to go beyond primitive guttural utterances.

While **visual communication** may be seen as separate from oral, it is likely that it developed originally because of the limitations in our speaking. Before words were first spoken, it is thought that drawings were used to explain things or record events. Ironically, once language had been created, much of the visual communication then became symbolic of the thing it described, rather than a true rendition of it.

It is estimated that a week's worth of news in an average newspaper contains more information than anyone in the eighteenth century would have learned in his or her lifetime.

Something to Think About . . .

While suffering from locked-in syndrome, a condition in which a patient is aware and awake but cannot move or communicate verbally due to complete paralysis of nearly all voluntary muscles in the body, Jean-Dominique Bauby managed to write his autobiography, *The Diving Bell and the Butterfly*, by blinking his left eye.

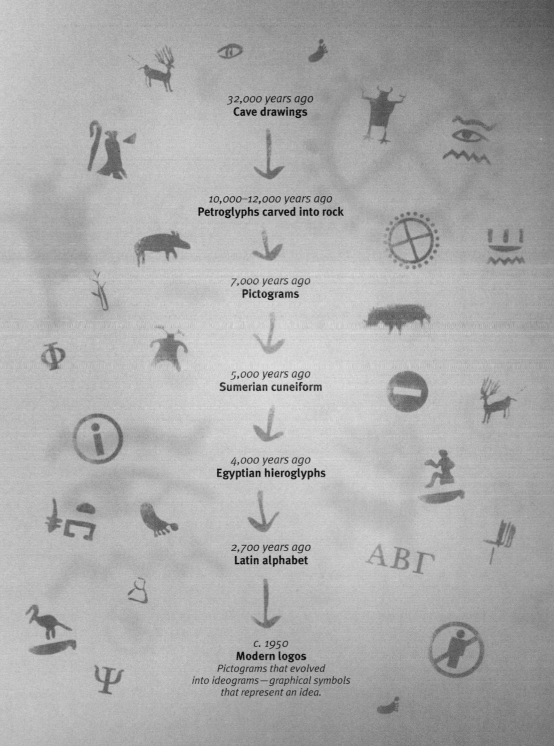

32,000 years ago
Cave drawings

10,000–12,000 years ago
Petroglyphs carved into rock

7,000 years ago
Pictograms

5,000 years ago
Sumerian cuneiform

4,000 years ago
Egyptian hieroglyphs

2,700 years ago
Latin alphabet

c. 1950
Modern logos
Pictograms that evolved
into ideograms—graphical symbols
that represent an idea.

How a Telephone Works_

Although phones—and cell phones—have changed quite dramatically from an aesthetic point over the past sixty years, the technology of how they work has essentially remained the same.

A telephone works by converting sound waves into an **electric current**, sending that current down a wire, and then converting it back into **sound waves**. In essence, it is no different from two cans and a piece of string, but it is more efficient and can work over much longer—almost infinite—distances.

With the cans method, the vibrations in the air created by your voice make the end of the can vibrate. This minute vibration is carried by the string to the can at the other end, causing it to vibrate in the same way, thus creating the same sound waves you created by speaking. The tighter the piece of string, the better the transmission will be.

A telephone replicates this idea. The end of the can is replaced by a **membrane** and **carbon granules**. When you speak, the **sound waves move the membrane**, which is attached to an electric circuit. The movement of the membrane changes the current in this circuit and it is this "electrical message" that is sent down the phone wire.

When you dial a number and someone answers, in effect they are **completing an electric circuit**. This allows your electrical message to travel along the wire and act on the membrane in the earpiece, reversing the process from your mouthpiece and turning the electric signal back into sound waves.

Although technology has come a long way and we no longer have a physical wire that connects the people at either end, the principle is the same: sound waves are turned into radio signals, these are then sent to the receiver, which converts them back into sound waves.

Something to Think About . . .

With phone handsets halving in size every eighteen months on average, scientists predict that, by the year 2017, cell phone designs will reach the physical limits of technology.

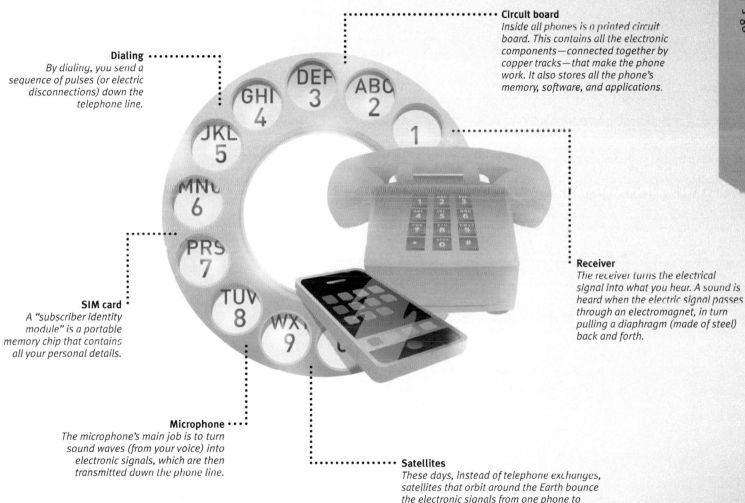

While the look and feel of most modern cell phones and smartphones may appear different from the original rotary-dial telephones, much of the technology that enables a conversation to take place is the same.

Circuit board
Inside all phones is a printed circuit board. This contains all the electronic components—connected together by copper tracks—that make the phone work. It also stores all the phone's memory, software, and applications.

Dialing
By dialing, you send a sequence of pulses (or electric disconnections) down the telephone line.

Receiver
The receiver turns the electrical signal into what you hear. A sound is heard when the electric signal passes through an electromagnet, in turn pulling a diaphragm (made of steel) back and forth.

SIM card
A "subscriber identity module" is a portable memory chip that contains all your personal details.

Microphone
The microphone's main job is to turn sound waves (from your voice) into electronic signals, which are then transmitted down the phone line.

Satellites
These days, instead of telephone exchanges, satellites that orbit around the Earth bounce the electronic signals from one phone to another. Telephone poles do this as well.

The first commercial text message was sent in December 1992. Today the number of text messages sent and received each day exceeds the total population of the planet.

08.6 The Satellites in Orbit_

The world changed forever on October 4, 1957. The change wasn't necessarily obvious to everyone at the time, but the implications of the successful launch and positioning of the satellite **Sputnik** were immense. In effect, it sounded the starting pistol for the **1960s space race** between the United States and the Soviet Union, led to the first Moon landing, and changed how we live and communicate. It also made the world much smaller.

Sputnik was the size of a beach ball, about 23 inches in diameter. Designed by a Soviet team headed by Sergei Korolev, it simply sent a beeping sound back to Earth for twenty-three days until its battery ran out. The beep could be picked up all around Earth as the shiny orb passed overhead. It continued to orbit Earth, with each orbit taking 96 minutes and 12 seconds, until it burned up when it reentered the atmosphere on January 4, 1958.

Since *Sputnik* first broke out of our atmosphere and flew above us, nearly 7,000 satellites (both **low-orbiting** and **geostationary**) have been launched. Of these, around 3,000 are orbiting Earth, relaying data and monitoring the planet. The main activities of these are weather monitoring, communications, scientific research, navigation, Earth observation, and military surveillance. Wherever you are now and whatever you are doing, someone, somewhere will be able to see you or hear you. Whether you're on your cell phone, using your car's navigation system, or just watching a big sporting event on television, you are not alone.

Something to Think About . . .

By the time *Sputnik* had come back down to Earth, the Soviet Union had already launched its successor, *Sputnik 2*, on November 7, 1957. This was a bigger satellite and contained the first live animal to be sent out of our atmosphere. It was a dog, reportedly a Laika breed, a stray found on the streets of Moscow.

What satellites are used for

Earth observation/remote sensing *9%*

Navigation *8%*

Military surveillance *7%*

Astrophysics/space science *5%*

Earth science/meteorology *4%*

Other *7%*

Communication *59%*

(All figures from UCS Satellite Database, 2010.)

08.7 The Age of Personal Computers_

In 1950 **computer scientist Alan Turing** predicted that, by the turn of the millennium, computers would have a billion bytes of memory—a preposterous statement at the time. Today, a 32-gigabyte smartphone has approximately **32 billion bytes of memory**.

With the invention of the microchip, almost anything became possible for the computer, and as their size has reduced, their speed has increased—there are almost no limits to what a computer can do. In 1974 the first "real" Intel-made processor (a computer runs on microchips), the 8080, had 2,500 transistors. By 2004 the Intel 2 had 592 million transistors!

MIPS (millions of instructions per second), the number of instructions that a computer can process in a second, is arguably **the best indicator of a computer's speed** and shows how, since the invention of the first personal computer, computers have excelled in speed, function, and memory.

Alan Turing's dream of **true artificial intelligence** has almost come to fruition, and it will not be long before computers start inventing better versions of themselves. Science fiction and science fact are, it seems, coming closer together.

Something to Think About . . .

Gordon E. Moore was one of the founders of Intel—the largest semiconductor chip maker in the world. In 1965 he noted that the number of components used in a single computer chip doubled every year, and saw no reason why this trend should not continue for at least ten years. In 1975 he altered this to be a doubling every *two years*. **"Moore's law"** is both a statement and a target for hardware development in all sorts of areas, from the number of transistors on a chip to the number of pixels in digital cameras.

The speed and development of the PC is shown by this graph showing the MIPS (millions of instructions per second) for many of the major PC chips since 1974.

Intel 8080 *0.5*
1974—The first "real" PC chip.

Motorola 68000 *1.0*
1979—Apple Mac's processor.

Intel 286 *2.66*
1982—The MS-DOS PC chip.

Intel 386DX *11.4*
1985

Motorola 68040 *44*
1990

Intel 486DX *54*
1992—Brought point-and-click to reality.

Motorola 68060 *88*
1994—Higher-end Macs and workstations.

Intel Pentium Pro *541*
1996—The beginning of the gaming PC.

Intel Pentium III *1,354*
1999—High-quality graphics.

AMD Athlon *3,561*
2000—The first 1 GHz PC chip.

Intel Pentium 4 Extreme *9,726*
2003—20,000 times faster than the 8080.

IBM Xenon Triple Core *19,200*
2005—Used in the Xbox 360.

Intel Core 2 Extreme *59,455*
2008—64-bit multicore processing

Intel Core i7 Extreme *147,600*
2010—Where to next?

The Growth of the Internet_

The **World Wide Web** has been in existence since the end of 1991 thanks to **Sir Tim Berners-Lee**. The latest estimate of the number of Web pages in existence is over 25 billion, although that has changed since you started reading this sentence. There are just under 7 billion people on the planet, so that comes out to three pages each.

If each page were a piece of standard letter-size paper and they were all stacked in a pile, that pile would be 1,553 miles high—the distance from Glasgow to Rome.

Something to Think About . . .

The first Web page was:

http://www.w3.org/History/19921103-hypertext/hypertext/WWW/TheProject.html

It has no pictures and downloads in 1 nanosecond.

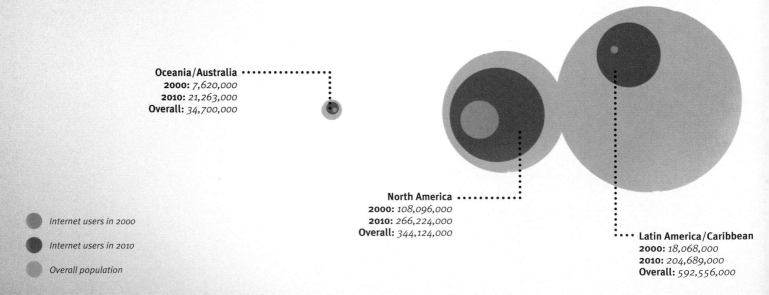

Oceania/Australia
2000: *7,620,000*
2010: *21,263,000*
Overall: *34,700,000*

North America
2000: *108,096,000*
2010: *266,224,000*
Overall: *344,124,000*

Latin America/Caribbean
2000: *18,068,000*
2010: *204,689,000*
Overall: *592,556,000*

Internet users in 2000

Internet users in 2010

Overall population

Around 210 billion e-mails are sent daily, an estimated 80 percent of which are spam.

While the number of people with access to the Internet is undoubtedly growing, this chart shows that there is still a large percentage of the population on each continent who don't have access.

Africa
2000: *4,514,400*
2010: *110,931,000*
Overall: *1,013,779,000*

Asia
2000: *114,304,000*
2010: *825,094,000*
Overall: *3,834,792,000*

Middle East
2000: *3,284,800*
2010: *63,240,000*
Overall: *212,336,000*

In 2010 there were an average of 31 billion searches on Google every month.

Europe
2000: *105,096,000*
2010: *475,069,000*
Overall: *813,319,000*

To reach a market audience of 50 million people, it took the Internet just four years. By comparison, it took television 13 years and radio 38 years.

08.9 The World of Social Networking_

If there was someone you went to school with but with whom you had lost touch, it is now possible, ridiculously easy in fact, to get in contact with him or her thanks to the phenomenon of social networking. With the Internet potentially connecting everyone to anyone, no one person is more than a couple of clicks away.

The concept of **six degrees of separation**, whereby we are all linked to everyone else by no more than six other people, or "links," has been proven beyond doubt with the rise of sites such as **Facebook**, **Twitter**, and **Myspace**. Not only can you locate that long-lost friend from school, it is now possible to feel that you are best friends with celebrities, politicians, or anyone on the planet.

The **first social networking site** is considered to be www.classmates.com. It was launched in 1995 and is still going strong. It has been overtaken by others, and all social networking sites are overshadowed by Facebook.

Twitter is the latest big arrival and is slightly different from the others. It allows users to give their opinions and comments on anything, but limits each statement to just 140 characters. Because followers spawn other followers, it has grown at an incredible rate.

Something to Think About . . .

Over 500 billion minutes are spent by users on Facebook each month. That's an average of forty-six minutes a day per active user.

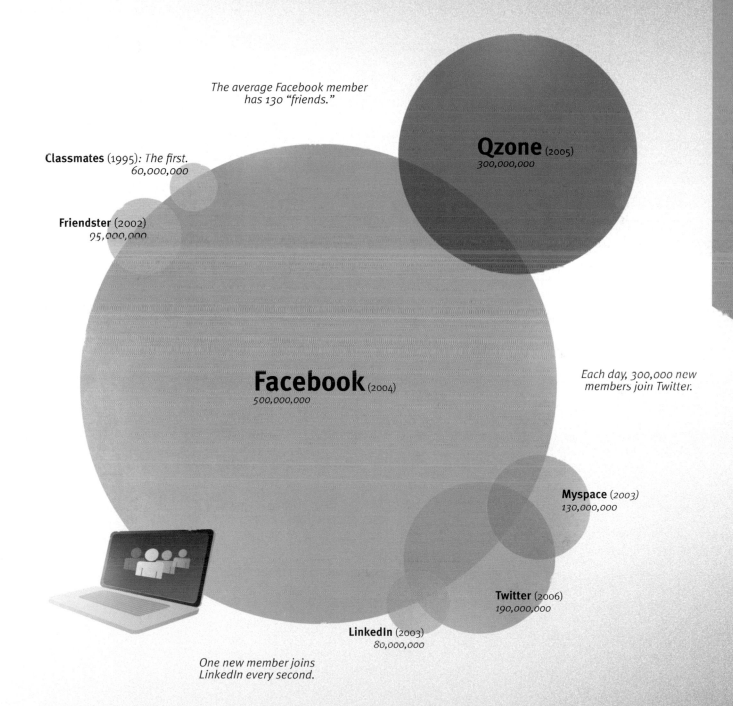

The average Facebook member has 130 "friends."

Qzone (2005)
300,000,000

Classmates (1995): *The first.*
60,000,000

Friendster (2002)
95,000,000

Each day, 300,000 new members join Twitter.

Facebook (2004)
500,000,000

Myspace (2003)
130,000,000

Twitter (2006)
190,000,000

LinkedIn (2003)
80,000,000

One new member joins LinkedIn every second.

Traveling Through Space_

In April 1950, a new comic strip hit the streets in England. Created and drawn by Frank Hampson, who had seen German rockets during World War II, it chronicled the adventures of Dan Dare, the Pilot of the Future. It was a fictional story set in 1995, and the first voyage was to Venus in a desperate bid to find a new source of food for Earth as our resources ran out.

Hampson was ahead of the game. No human being has traveled farther than the Moon, but in principle Hampson was right. It was the German expertise, shared between the Soviet Union and the United States, that was the driving force for **space exploration**.

The cost of space exploration is immense, and so, since men first landed on the Moon, the costs have been kept down by sending unmanned craft. In addition to the voyages to faraway planets, the images gathered by the **Hubble Space Telescope** have enriched our knowledge of what is out there. In some ways we have learned more from the Hubble than we have from the much more distant missions. The images it receives come from way beyond the distance that any satellite has traveled.

Discussions are now in process again about trying to send humans to another planet. As our finite resources begin to deplete, this may be because of actual need rather than just a thirst for knowledge.

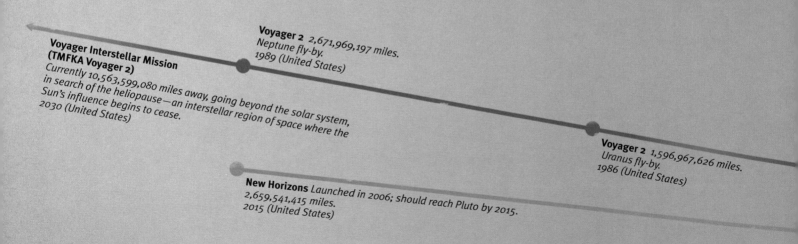

Voyager 2 2,671,969,197 miles.
Neptune fly-by.
1989 (United States)

**Voyager Interstellar Mission
(TMFKA Voyager 2)**
Currently 10,563,599,080 miles away, going beyond the solar system,
in search of the heliopause—an interstellar region of space where the
Sun's influence begins to cease.
2030 (United States)

Voyager 2 1,596,967,626 miles.
Uranus fly-by.
1986 (United States)

New Horizons Launched in 2006; should reach Pluto by 2015.
2,659,541,415 miles.
2015 (United States)

Distances traveled of man-made crafts away from Earth
(Minimum distances used for orbital trajectories.)

Pioneer 11 745,665,317 miles.
Saturn fly-by.
1979 (United States)

Pioneer 10 554,899,646 miles.
Jupiter fly-by.
1973 (United States)

Something to Think About . . .

Only twelve men have walked on the surface of the Moon. The first to set foot on the surface was Neil Armstrong on July 21, 1969; the last was Eugene Cernan on December 14, 1972.

Venera 7 23,737,029 miles.
Landed on Venus.
1970 (Soviet Union)

Apollo 11 233,861 miles.
Manned spacecraft, landed on the Moon.
1969 (Neil Armstrong, Buzz Aldrin, United States)

Vostok 1 203 miles. First human spaceflight.
1961 (Yury Gagarin, Soviet Union)

Sputnik 587 miles.
1957 (Soviet Union)

Mars 2 34,176,350 miles.
Landed on Mars.
1972 (Soviet Union)

Mariner 10 47,846,890 miles.
Mercury fly-by.
1974 (United States)

Hubble Space Telescope 342 miles; in orbit.
1990 (United States)

International Space Station 218 miles, in orbit.
1998 (Various countries)

How Times Have Changed_

Life has changed beyond all recognition over the last sixty years and yet much has stayed the same. Over the past few years, businesses and employers have seen a massive growth in the Internet and telecommunications, and improved access to travel, making the working day simpler and easier for employees.

In most developed countries in the 1950s, daily life was based very much around the immediate family and the home. It was easier to split the day into the three traditional segments of **sleep**, **work**, and **leisure**. Due mainly to improvements in **medicine**, **nutrition**, and **living standards**, people are living, on average, ten years longer in developed nations. On the surface this should be a good thing, but it has problems.

With a **longer life expectancy**, the average age of the population has risen and this generally means that, as a percentage of the population as a whole, there are more people not working. This puts an increased burden on the working population as they try to support the young and the retired. While the number of hours at work in developed countries has remained almost constant—about eight hours a day—it is clear that time actually spent working has decreased due to the growth of the Internet and improved global telecommunications.

Something to Think About . . .

In the developed world in the 1950s, only 10 percent of households had a telephone. In the mid-1950s, less than 30 percent of homes in the developed world had television sets. Today, more than 85 percent of homes in the developed world have digital television sets.

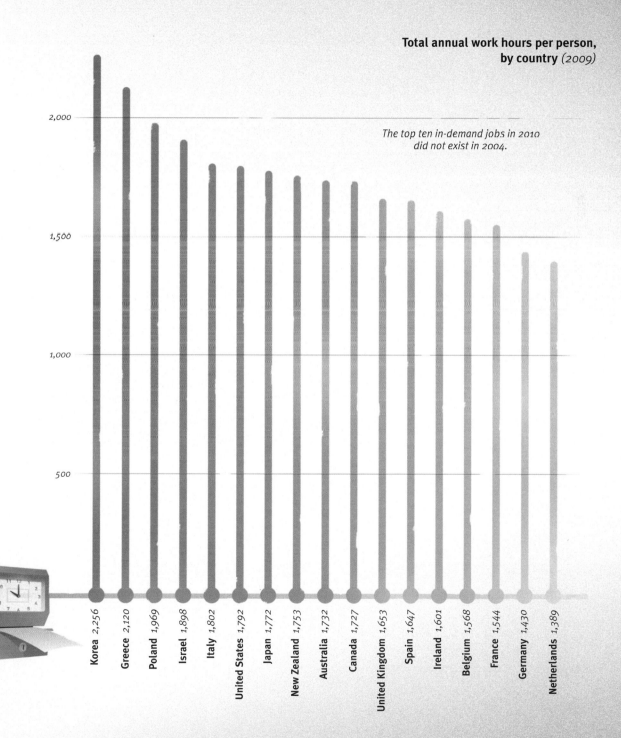

**Total annual work hours per person,
by country** *(2009)*

*The top ten in-demand jobs in 2010
did not exist in 2004.*

2,000

1,500

1,000

500

Korea *2,256*
Greece *2,120*
Poland *1,969*
Israel *1,898*
Italy *1,802*
United States *1,792*
Japan *1,772*
New Zealand *1,753*
Australia *1,732*
Canada *1,727*
United Kingdom *1,653*
Spain *1,647*
Ireland *1,601*
Belgium *1,568*
France *1,544*
Germany *1,430*
Netherlands *1,389*

What Happens Next?

This book has looked at our planet, ourselves, and the way we live, covering everything from the big bang right up to today. The one thing we cannot say with any certainty is what is going to happen tomorrow. Pessimists predict that **global warming** will eventually make life in most places impossible, that Earth's **natural resources** will run out, and we will meet the same fate as the dinosaurs, to die out as a species and eventually be replaced. The optimists look at what humans have achieved in our relatively short time on this globe and suggest that whatever happens, we will find a way to survive. It may require that we all journey to another planet, or it may mean finding a safe **alternative to fossil fuels** and a way to feed an **ever-growing population** without depleting the oxygen-giving rain forests.

We've all come a long way since that single, unifying moment 13.7 billion years ago that brought everything into being, but what we don't know is where we are on the journey. It is an overused cliché to say that if the life of this planet were to be broken down into a single day, we are already at 23 hours, 59 minutes, and 59 seconds, but no one really knows.

As a species, we may not know what will happen tomorrow, but we have it in our power to shape what happens—and it is this one significant fact that has made us different from the other living things that share our planet. We can make decisions that affect everything—but can we overcome our faults in order to do what is best?

The choice is yours, but it could affect everyone's future.

Something to Think About . . .

The world uses 85 million barrels of oil per day. A barrel is 35 gallons, so that is 0.4 gallon per person per day.

Things of the future to look forward to—or not

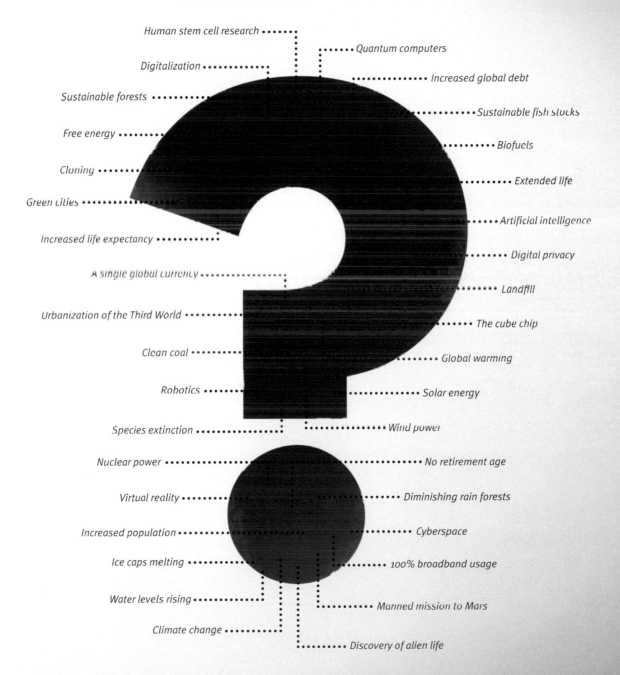

Human stem cell research

Quantum computers

Digitalization

Increased global debt

Sustainable forests

Sustainable fish stocks

Free energy

Biofuels

Cloning

Extended life

Green cities

Artificial intelligence

Increased life expectancy

Digital privacy

A single global currency

Landfill

Urbanization of the Third World

The cube chip

Clean coal

Global warming

Robotics

Solar energy

Species extinction

Wind power

Nuclear power

No retirement age

Virtual reality

Diminishing rain forests

Increased population

Cyberspace

Ice caps melting

100% broadband usage

Water levels rising

Manned mission to Mars

Climate change

Discovery of alien life

Index_

Index_ *cont.*

Daniel Tatarsky

Daniel was born in Liverpool, England, and now lives in London with his wife. His first book was *Flick to Kick: An Illustrated History of Subbuteo*. He is the consultant editor for Orion Books' Eagle publishing program and is the author of a biography of Eagle's cover star, Dan Dare.

He came up with the title *Everything You Need to Know About Everything You Need to Know About* over breakfast one morning and is delighted it has now reached fruition. His favorite discoveries while writing the book were the details of the invention of the bread-slicing machine and the resulting effect this had on bread consumption. He now agrees with the old adage that the invention of sliced bread is indeed a benchmark against which all other inventions should be measured.

Acknowledgments

I would like to thank Katie Cowan and Malcolm Croft for helping me turn a title into a fully fledged book.

For the design of the book, I am indebted to Zoe Anspach for getting the ball rolling in the right direction and to Steve Russell for picking up the baton and running with it in marvelous fashion. Steve's contribution has spanned design, illustration, and content, and we could not have produced this book without him. Thanks also to Katie Hewett and Chris Stone for their eagle-eyed editing and sage guidance.

Finally, I would like to dedicate this book to my dad, Malcolm, who left school at thirteen but knew more than anyone I know and thus always beat me and my brothers at trivia games. And also to my mother, Emmie, who genuinely believes that she knows everything about everything.

Steve Russell

Illustrator/Designer

Steve was born and bred in Auckland, New Zealand. He has been based in London since 2006, where he works as a freelance designer and illustrator.

When first approached to illustrate and design *Everything You Need to Know About Everything You Need to Know About,* he wasn't sure if he was qualified, but looking over his portfolio of work he realized that he has designed books on just every subject imaginable—photography, tattoos, street art, cool caravans, war posters, ocean liners, ornithology, sports, design, architecture, grammar guides, Tongan proverbs, Maori language textbooks, children's books, a Japanese textbook, and a book about New Zealand hip-hop. So he thought he would give it a go.

When Steve is not designing, you can find him enjoying live gigs around London, pretending to be a photographer, or traveling. An avid traveler, so far his travels have taken him to many weird and wonderful places, such as Easter Island, Syria, Albania, Iran, and Bolivia. He once played basketball with Tibetan monks and has been mistaken for a World Strongman competitor in China.

You can see more of his work at www.aka-designaholic.com.

Acknowledgments

I would like to thank everybody involved in this book—Daniel Tatarsky, Katie Cowan, and especially Malcolm Croft for putting up with my endless phone calls, questions, requests, and demands.

I would also like to thank Georgina Hewitt for hooking me up with Anova and also say a big thank-you to all my friends for putting up with me while I spent endless hours working on this book.

This book is dedicated to my mother, Margot Russell, because everything worthwhile I do will always be dedicated to her.